PRAISE FOR
TRAVELING BY A DIFFERENT WAY

"...Well informed, insightful biblical interpretation..."
—Carl R. Holladay, C. H. Candler Professor Emeritus of New Testament, Emory University

"With his trademark combination of humility and brilliance, Joel Huffstetler invites us to see a deeply troubled world through the eyes of grace and redemption. It's a perspective we desperately needed during the COVID pandemic. It's a perspective we desperately need today."
—Jeff Ringer, Associate Professor of English, University of Tennessee

"Reading these meditations, which both comfort and challenge, I find them just as relevant as when I first heard them offered as sermons during the pandemic. Huffstetler points to God's abiding presence with us even in the midst of the uncertainties of life during the pandemic with all its attending chaos. He reminds us that we need not be overcome by fear even in the midst of the most challenging of times."
—Denise King, Provost (retired), Big Sandy Community and Technical College

"Set during the pandemic, Fr. Joel carefully guides his worried

congregation through these deeply thought-provoking and engaging sermons which remain relevant for all times and places."
—Brenda Orcutt, Member of Oil Painters of America, American Impressionist Society, and American Women Artists

∽

"Joel Huffstetler's *Traveling By A Different Way* is an excellent source of inspiration. I highly recommend it."
—Wesley H. Wachob, author of *The Voice of Jesus in the Social Rhetoric of James* (Cambridge University Press)

TRAVELING BY A DIFFERENT WAY

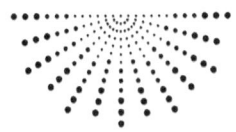

JOEL W. HUFFSTETLER

Apocryphile Press
PO Box 255
Hannacroix, NY 12087
www.apocryphilepress.com

Copyright © 2025 by Joel W. Huffstetler
Printed in the United States of America
ISBN 978-1-965646-51-9 | paper
ISBN 978-1-965646-52-6 | ePub

Cover image, *Positive Energy*, Oil on Canvas, by Brenda Orcutt.
www.orcuttfineart.com

Scripture quotations are from the New Revised Standard Version Bible, © 1989 National Council of the Churches of Christ in the United States of America. Used by permission. All rights reserved worldwide.

No part of this book may be reproduced, stored in a retrieval system, or transmitted in any form or by any means—electronic, mechanical, photocopy, recording, or otherwise—without written permission of the author and publisher, except for brief quotations in printed reviews.

Please join our mailing list at www.apocryphilepress.com/free. We'll keep you up-to-date on all our new releases, and we'll also send you a FREE BOOK. Visit us today!

*To Donna Jane and Carl Holladay,
with lasting gratitude*

CONTENTS

Foreword — ix
Preface — xiii
Introduction — xv

1. Traveling By A Different Way — 1
2. Can Anything Good Come Out of Nazareth? — 6
3. The Rhythm of Habit — 11
4. Thunderstruck — 15
5. A Mixture of Awe and Terror — 21
6. The Unmistakable Voice that Matters — 27
7. In the Light of Easter — 33
8. A Truth that Transcends the Pandemic — 38
9. Deep Roots, and Yet... — 43
10. Christ Is in Our Midst! — 49
11. The Essence of the Gospel — 54
12. I See You — 59
13. As Clear as It Gets — 64
14. The Spirit Blows Where It Chooses — 70
15. Fighting for Human Rights on Earth — 76
16. A Time of Soul Searching for Us All — 81
17. One of the Glory Days of the Christian Year — 87
18. The Bracing Challenge of a New Way of Life — 94
19. A Strong Sense of Self — 99
20. Compassion — 105
21. One Phone Call Away — 112
22. The Ministers—All of the People — 118
23. Is It Loving? — 125
24. Watch How You Walk — 131
25. Stand Firm — 136
26. Action Consonant with Conviction — 144
27. The Sin of Discrimination — 152

28. Taming the Tongue — 157
29. Wisdom from Above — 162
30. Welcome to the Church of the Future — 168
31. The Saddest Verse in the Bible — 175
32. Widening the Circle — 181
33. The Value of Time — 186
34. The Dance of Contrition and Joy — 191
35. A Moment of Truth — 196
36. The Slender Thread of Mary's Response — 201

Acknowledgments — 205
About the Author — 207

FOREWORD

What do you get when well-informed, insightful biblical interpretation joins closely observed life experience in addressing a congregation trying to cope with the pandemic during 2021? Thirty-six engaging sermons preached by Joel Huffstetler, Rector of St. Luke's Episcopal Church in Cleveland, Tennessee.

The titles themselves are enticing: The Rhythm of Habit; Deep Roots, and Yet; As Clear as It Gets; One Phone Call Away; The Value of Time; The Dance of Contrition and Joy; The Slender Thread of Mary's Response. The sermons retain their conversational tone, revealing a confident, experienced pastor speaking candidly to his congregation about the day-to-day challenges they are facing. They are asking: When will an effective vaccine be available? How long will we have to wear masks? When will we again experience each other's presence face-to-face as a vigorous, interactive congregation of believers?

The preacher takes these questions seriously, while acknowledging the toll the pandemic is taking on congregational life. Change and technological innovation set in as an "online church" begins to take shape. Never doubting the damaging effects of the pandemic, Huffstetler helps his church see how the nature of its ministry is changing. Gradually an audience without geographical boundaries begins to develop, and the preacher interprets this as a fresh opportunity to expand the church's mission far beyond its immediate vicinity. "Silver linings in the cloud," he calls it. An overarching theme is how good has come from this otherwise painful and unsettling time. "Welcome to the church of the future," he tells his parishioners.

A menacing threat to be sure, the pandemic is not the only thing his church has to deal with. Texts from the Letter of James prompt him to speak to broader social, political issues:

> We are living in a particularly tense time in our culture, a time of deep, seemingly intractable divisions. There is a growing fatigue from the pandemic. We all feel it. And there is rising anger. We are all increasingly on edge. [Now] words are more important to us than ever. The stakes regarding our use of the gift of speech are as high as at any other point in our lifetimes.

Especially remarkable is how Huffstetler orchestrates their response to these challenges. One of his key strengths is the effective use of simple, direct prose. The reader is allowed to listen in on an intimate conversation in which the preacher engages in biblical exposition with his congregation. He gives succinct quotations from a wide variety of biblical commentaries that allow him to clinch a particular point. Here we see him gradually educating his congregation in the use of solid biblical scholarship.

Huffstetler freely tells stories from his own experience growing up in North Carolina, and from his decades of pastoral experience in different places, but they are unfailingly apt in illustrating his point. And yet, he manages to avoid self-promotion, following his own advice: "preach to yourself, not of yourself." Typically the stories align the preacher with the congregation, so that both are experiencing the truth of the gospel together. "We are all on the journey of faith together," he reminds them. He also shows them how to see the world through the eyes of faith: palm trees in the Florida panhandle bending without breaking during a violent storm to illuminate what "being willing to yield" means in James 3:17.

Notable is his gift of selecting memorable lines: "The main thing is to keep the main thing the main thing." Well-chosen lines from a variety of notables such as Augustine, Rumi, Søren Kierkegaard, Karl Barth, Michael Mayne, even Dean Smith, not only reflect the preacher's wide reading but also show him acquainting his congregation with a larger literary and theological world. Here, as elsewhere, he allows his congregation to hear a rich variety of ancient and modern voices from different social contexts interpreting Scripture and grappling with complex doctrinal issues.

In all these sermons, we hear an imaginative, theologically astute preacher and life observer relate the Bible and the Christian faith meaningfully to a congregation and its wider online audience who are struggling to make sense of an ongoing health crisis and a complex mix of social issues over the course of a year.

Carl R. Holladay
C. H. Candler Professor Emeritus
of New Testament, Emory University
Durham, NC
January 4, 2025

PREFACE

In the early days of the COVID-19 pandemic we were told that it was necessary to follow pandemic protocols, including 'lock down,' for "a few weeks" in order to help "flatten the curve" of hospitalizations. In reality, those 'few weeks' of following emergency protocols became a few months, and, eventually, more than a year. Like 2020, 2021 will also be remembered as a plague year.

In addition to the COVID-19 emergency, the social protests following the deaths of Ahmaud Arbery, George Floyd and Breonna Taylor added fuel to the fire of an already stressful time. In his literary biography of the Christian writer Frederick Buechner, Jeffrey Munroe, in reflecting on Buechner's activities and commitments during the 1960s, writes: "America erupted in the 1960s..." America erupted again in the early 2020s.

The biblical meditations contained in this collection come from the year 2021. First offered in St. Luke's Episcopal Church in Cleveland, Tennessee, all have been revised for publication. While each address was first crafted to meet a particular moment in the life of a particular Christian congregation, they were also offered with a view to the future, asking both preacher and hearer: What are the lessons we are meant to be learning during these turbulent times? What changes in our ways of thinking and acting are we being called to make? Are there silver linings to be discerned amidst the myriad challenges none of us would have chosen to face? To put it in more obviously theological terms, each address was meant to face the question: How can this time be redeemed? Or, put another way: Going forward, are we being called to travel by a different way?

Joel W. Huffstetler
Rector, St. Luke's Episcopal Church
Cleveland, Tennessee
Ascension Day 2025

INTRODUCTION

The best books of sermons never begin with the purpose of being a book. Rather, each sermon begins with a preacher and a Christian community gathered to hear Good News. Does *that* sermon work? If so, might the sermon which edified and inspired a people in a certain time and place also be a source of Good News to the reader who is now 'overhearing' the sermon from a distance?

I believe Joel Huffstetler's newest collection of sermons from the pandemic year of 2021 will be the kind of book that will be well worth 'overhearing' now. These are biblical sermons which also engaged the on-the-ground realities of community life in the lingering months of the pandemic. In Christian communities, our primary context is that of a people of the Book, a people shaped by Holy Scripture. From that context, we situate ourselves in the local physical communities where we live and work, experiencing both joy and sorrow. Fr. Joel is faithful to both communities and has fashioned sermons that will continue to bless many readers who have never set foot in St. Luke's Episcopal Church in Cleveland, Tennessee.

The monk Thomas Merton shared this wisdom in his classic book *New Seeds of Contemplation:*

We do not go into the desert to escape people but to learn how to find them; we do not leave them in order to have nothing more to do with them, but to find out the way to do them the most good. But this is only a secondary end. The one end that includes all others is the love of God.

He is making the case that a true contemplative must have perspective and a healthy understanding of themselves as a person made in God's image before entering into community with others. Otherwise, as I recall hearing a Baptist preacher say, "We end up using people and loving things, not loving people and using things."

Fr. Joel is a priest, pastor, teacher, and preacher who lives deeply in the context of Holy Scripture. He goes into those biblical stories, however, not to avoid people or the matters of our time. Rather, it is his ongoing engagement of the biblical narrative that shapes the wisdom which blessed the first hearers of these sermons in 2021 and will offer ongoing wisdom to all who will linger with these sermons going forward. If you choose to attend to them, you will be blessed.

Brian L. Cole
Fifth Bishop of the Episcopal Diocese of East Tennessee
Lent 2025

1
TRAVELING BY A DIFFERENT WAY

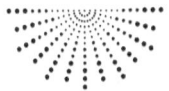

MATTHEW 2:1–12 • 3 JANUARY 2021
SECOND SUNDAY OF CHRISTMAS

¹In the time of King Herod, after Jesus was born in Bethlehem of Judea, wise men from the East came to Jerusalem, ²asking, "Where is the child who has been born king of the Jews? For we observed his star at its rising, and have come to pay him homage." ³When King Herod heard this, he was frightened, and all Jerusalem with him; ⁴and calling together all the chief priests and scribes of the people, he inquired of them where the Messiah was to be born. ⁵They told him, "In Bethlehem of Judea; for so it has been written by the prophet: ⁶'And you, Bethlehem, in the land of Judah, are by no means least among the rulers of Judah; for from you shall come a ruler who is to shepherd my people Israel.'" ⁷Then Herod secretly called for the wise men and learned from them the exact time when the star had appeared. ⁸Then he sent them to Bethlehem, saying, "Go and search diligently for the child; and when you have found him, bring me word so that I may also go and pay him homage." ⁹When they had heard the king, they set out; and there, ahead of them, went the star that they had seen at its rising, until it stopped over the place where the child

was. ¹⁰When they saw that the star had stopped, they were overwhelmed with joy. ¹¹On entering the house, they saw the child with Mary his mother; and they knelt down and paid him homage. Then, opening their treasure chests, they offered him gifts of gold, frankincense, and myrrh. ¹²And having been warned in a dream not to return to Herod, they left for their own country by another road.

~

Ever since I was a child I have enjoyed looking at Christmas lights. I *really* enjoy looking at Christmas lights. Debbie and I always mark out a couple of evenings each December to ride around town and take in as many Christmas lights as possible. Most years, I see at least one Nativity scene that particularly catches my attention. The scene typically includes Mary, Joseph, the baby Jesus, some quite clean looking shepherds, some exceptionally well-behaved sheep, the wise men—and Santa Claus!

The New Testament contains four canonical Gospels which offer four different perspectives on the life and meaning of Jesus. The four Gospels share much in common, of course, but each is distinctive as well. Matthew, Mark, Luke and John each has its own distinct point of view. Imagine if I were to hand out a fresh legal pad to four of you and said: "Take your time, and write as much or as little as you like on who Jesus Christ is to you." Imagine four of you in the congregation taking on this assignment. Doubtless there would be points of commonality in what was written, and yet there would also be distinctions. Each of the four would write from her or his own perspective. And that is what we have in the Gospels: four distinct stories of Jesus. Mark and John chose not to include infancy narratives in their Gospels, thus we get our Christmas stories from Matthew and Luke. Though Matthew's infancy narrative is of invaluable importance to the Christian tradition, Luke's is more familiar in popular culture. A portion of Luke's infancy narrative is recited by Linus in "A Charlie Brown Christmas." Case closed.

That said, it is only in Matthew's Gospel that we encounter the Magi, the wise men. "Magi" comes from the Greek word for magic. You will notice that Matthew does not tell us the names (nor the number!) of the Magi. The names Gaspar, Melchior, and Balthasar are supplied by later tradition. Matthew does not say that they were kings, and in fact, they almost certainly were not kings. They were in all probability philosophers, magicians, astrologers—sages. These Magi looked to the heavens for signs, for meaning. Matthew does tell us that they came from the East and, given the historical context, in all likelihood came from either modern-day Iraq, Iran, or Saudi Arabia.

One of the great preachers of our time is Sam Lloyd, who was chaplain at the University of the South when I was a student in the seminary there. In a fine collection of sermons from his time as dean of Washington National Cathedral (2005–11), Sam Lloyd states in a sermon titled, "The Magi and Us": "For Matthew, the story of the Magi is *the* Christmas story, the arrival of Gentiles from the far corners of the earth to worship the next king."[1] One of the distinctives of Matthew is that it is regarded as the most Jewish of the four Gospels. There are frequent Old Testament references in Matthew, and much of its content is portrayed as having "fulfilled" the Scriptures. Matthew's Gospel offers a thoroughgoingly Jewish perspective, and yet *the* Christmas story he tells has to do with *Gentiles* and their recognition that this newborn child will come to be recognized as the king of the Jews.

Our text is Matthew 2:1–12. If we go all the way to the end of Matthew, we read the risen Christ saying in 28:19: "Go therefore and make disciples of *all* (emphasis added) nations, baptizing them in the name of the Father and of the Son and of the Holy Spirit..." The Great Commission, the climactic ending of the Gospel of Matthew, once again involves Gentiles. Post-Easter, the risen Christ is Lord of all, yet even in the beginning of his Gospel, through the story of the Magi, Matthew would have us understand that this particular Jewish child is destined to bring good news to all humanity.

In addition to the Magi, we meet King Herod in our passage. Herod was a native 'client' king, a puppet king who ruled at the pleasure of Rome. Sam Lloyd says of King Herod: "Herod is...one of history's worst villains. He murdered his wife, three of his children, and most of his good friends—anyone who made him feel threatened."[2] I would add to Lloyd's list that Herod also murdered his mother-in-law, his brother-in-law, and an uncle. Herod was a merciless tyrant. In a summary statement, N. T. Wright says of Herod: "The house of Herod did not take kindly to the idea of anyone else claiming to be 'king of the Jews.'"[3]

We read in 2:11: "On entering the house, [the Magi] saw the child with Mary his mother; and they knelt down and paid him homage. Then, opening their treasure chests, they offered him gifts of gold, frankincense, and myrrh." And then in 2:12: "And having been warned in a dream not to return to Herod, they left for their own country by another road."

Sermons offered during this pandemic need to connect to the real world concerns of hearers. Preaching is always meant to be authentic, grounded, but especially now, in such a turbulent time as ours, every word of every sermon should be carefully chosen for maximum impact. Reflecting on 2:12, Lloyd states: "to follow this child is to live [in] a different way."[4] The Magi had the wisdom to choose to go home by a different road, *a different way*. And for us to follow the Christ is to live our lives in a different way—even now in these especially challenging times. Reflecting on the place of spirituality in the pandemic, Rowan Williams has written in his new book, *Candles in the Dark: Faith, Hope and Love in a Time of Pandemic*: "The great question, as and when we have emerged from the immediate shadow of the pandemic, will be: What have we learned?"[5] Yet even while still in the throes of the pandemic, we are meant to consider what lastingly important spiritual lessons we can already be learning. How are our priorities being reshaped as we work our way through the pandemic? Our commitments? Our passion for justice and peace? In the end, what will we have learned? And how will we have been transformed for the better?

It has been over thirty years since I have heard Sam Lloyd preach in person. It is hard for me to believe that it has been that long, because in my mind's memory I can still hear the tone of his voice. I can still hear his inflections. And I can still remember many of the punchlines of Sam's sermons all these years later. Sam Lloyd took great care in preparing his sermons. It was clear each week that he had put in the requisite amount of time, study, and reflection—and on the day his delivery was as smooth as silk. Every week Sam's meticulously prepared sermons were delivered with precision, and with grace. In thinking this past week of Sam's preaching, I was reminded of something Sir Laurence Olivier said when asked: What is the key to a great performance? Olivier's answer: "The key to a great performance is having the humility to prepare, and then the confidence to pull it off." What an extraordinary insight. Sam Lloyd's preaching has that rare blend of humility and confidence, and in honor of all that he has taught me and so many others by example over the years, on this Second Sunday of Christmas I leave us with Sam's words: "We who have been to Bethlehem this season now face the question, Are we willing to follow this child? If so, we have quite an adventure ahead, traveling by a different way."[6] Amen.

---

1. Samuel T. Lloyd III, *Sermons from the National Cathedral: Soundings for the Journey* (Lanham, MD: Rowman & Littlefield Publishers, Inc., 2013), 248.
2. *Ibid.*, 249.
3. N. T. Wright, *Matthew for Everyone: Part One, Chapters 1–15.* Second Edition (Louisville: Westminster John Knox Press, 2004), 11.
4. Lloyd, 250.
5. Rowan Williams, *Candles In the Dark: Faith, Hope and Love In A Time of Pandemic* (London: Society for Promoting Christian Knowledge, 2020), 95.
6. Lloyd, 250.

2
CAN ANYTHING GOOD COME OUT OF NAZARETH?

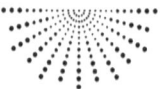

JOHN 1:43–51 • 17 JANUARY 2021
SECOND SUNDAY AFTER THE EPIPHANY

⁴³The next day Jesus decided to go to Galilee. He found Philip and said to him, "Follow me." ⁴⁴Now Philip was from Bethsaida, the city of Andrew and Peter. ⁴⁵Philip found Nathanael and said to him, "We have found him about whom Moses in the law and also the prophets wrote, Jesus son of Joseph from Nazareth." ⁴⁶Nathanael said to him, "Can anything good come out of Nazareth?" Philip said to him, "Come and see." ⁴⁷When Jesus saw Nathanael coming toward him, he said of him, "Here is truly an Israelite in whom there is no deceit!" ⁴⁸Nathanael asked him, "Where did you get to know me?" Jesus answered, "I saw you under the fig tree before Philip called you." ⁴⁹Nathanael replied, "Rabbi, you are the Son of God! You are the King of Israel!" ⁵⁰Jesus answered, "Do you believe because I told that I saw you under the fig tree? You will see greater things than these." ⁵¹And he said to him, "Very truly, I tell you, you will see heaven opened and the angels of God ascending and descending upon the Son of Man."

When we are first getting to know someone, it is common to ask: "Where are you from?" Or, as I would say: "Where you from?" I am from the southern Piedmont of North Carolina, and so I (we) typically drop the "are" in the question. And I drop the "e" from "where" *and* I pronounce "from" as *frum*. All of this is done unconsciously, and reflects the regional dialect I learned in my childhood. So "Where are you from?" for me is: "Wher' you *frum*?"

"Where are you from?" is a common conversation starter. A visitor to St. Luke's, who is now a beloved parishioner and friend, said to me the day of her first visit: "You're from North Carolina." Having just met her, I asked: "How do you know that?" She said, "Because you don't say *want*, you say *wont*." And she was right. If I wish to say, "I will not want to do that," what I actually say is: "I won't wont to do that."

Debbie and I were in Paris a number of years ago, and on a gloriously sunny day we paid a visit to the Rodin Museum. The grounds of the museum include a beautiful garden which features a number of Rodin's statues. During our visit, there came a point when I saw three men about my age whom I could hear talking to each other in English—*my* English. I could not help but overhear a certain twang which sounded so intimately familiar to me, and, being in *Paris*, I simply could not resist the temptation, and so I approached them slowly and said: "I don't ever do this, but y'all have got to be frum North Carolina." To which one of them replied: "We're frum Hick'ry (Hickory). Wher' you frum?" "I'm frum Gaston County." And from that moment we all talked as if we had known each other forever.

The question can be used differently. "Where are you from?" can be a way to determine how much we have in common, *or*, how we might be different. It can be a way of saying: "You're not from around here, are you?" We had a foreign exchange student from Sweden in the parish a couple of years ago. He had a real impact on our youth, and our youth had a similar impact on him. It was a wonderful, mutually beneficial relationship. At some point prior to him giving his Youth Sunday sermon he said to me in reference to his mother: "When she found out I was coming to Tennessee, she cried." I asked why, and he told me that she said: "I don't want you to be that close to Alabama." Which is hilarious in Tennessee, though not in Alabama.

When I was going away to college, I have a specific memory of being pulled aside by a loved one the day before I made the *two-hour* journey north to college, and she proceeded to tell me three things to be wary of regarding "Northerners." 1. They drink more than we do. 2. They are not as friendly as we are. 3. A lot of them are Catholic. The conversation was not subtle. I was to be wary of people from 'up North.' Of course it works both ways. Prejudice nearly always works both ways. When I was nearing graduation from college, a professor of sociology—which is key to this brief story—a professor of *sociology* came up to congratulate me on my academic accomplishments in the Social Sciences department, and in that brief conversation he said to me at one point: "Where are you from?" And I said: "I'm from (frum) Gaston County, North Carolina." He responded: "Well, originally, where are you from?" And I said: "I'm from North Carolina." To which he replied: "Oh, I'm surprised that you're a Southerner." Outright regional prejudice—from a highly esteemed professor of sociology.

We read the Bible with 2,000 years' worth of hindsight at our disposal. We have twenty centuries of history and interpretation to reflect upon. But the characters *in* the Bible were experiencing its events in real time, and thus Nathanael had no prior knowledge of Jesus before their first meeting recorded in John 1:47–51. From two millennia away we know more about Jesus than Nathanael did standing right in front of him.

Nazareth was an agrarian village of zero historical importance prior to its recognition as the hometown of Jesus. Nazareth, in the time of the New Testament, had no geographic significance and was of no strategic importance to the nation of Israel. To be from Nazareth was to be from 'nowhere.' And so Nathanael instinctively, reflexively, asks: "Can anything good come out of Nazareth?"

One of the great scholars of the Gospel of John was D. Moody Smith: Dwight Moody Smith, who taught for many years at Duke Divinity School. In his commentary on this encounter between Nathanael and Jesus, Smith writes: "Only being with Jesus provides sufficient basis to understand who he is."[1] A one-liner with such powerful insight. And *we* have to be with someone to get to know who they really are. We have to engage someone in conversation in order to gain an informed sense of what they stand for. Perhaps most important of all, we have to listen carefully in order to *hear*. We have to listen to someone, talk to them, and engage them with an open mind if we wish to get beyond our initial, instinctive, reflexive prejudgments. We all learned as children: "You cannot judge a book by its cover." And thus Smith's comment on John 1:46a: *Only being with Jesus provides sufficient basis to understand him.*

In thinking about Nathanael and his instinctive prejudice, especially in light of this particular period in our history, in preparing for this address I could not help but be reminded of the March on Washington, August 28, 1963. In the midst of his "I Have a Dream" speech, Dr. Martin Luther King, Jr. said: "I have a dream that my four little children will one day live in a nation where they will not be judged by the color of their skin but by the content of their character." Those words were spoken fifty-seven years ago.

Nathanael's being in the presence of Jesus results in this marvelous exchange in 1:47–49: "When Jesus saw Nathanael coming toward him, he said of him, 'Here is truly an Israelite in whom there is no deceit!' Nathanael asked him, 'Where did you get to know me?' Jesus answered, 'I saw you under the fig tree before Philip called you.' Nathanael replied, 'Rabbi, you are the Son of God! You are the King of Israel!'" From *Can anything good come out of Nazareth?* Nathanael's whole sense of Jesus is turned around by what? By engagement, by conversation. Nathanael felt seen, understood, valued—and in the process his whole sense, his whole perception of Jesus was turned from dismissive to respectful. "Rabbi, you are the Son of God! You are the King of Israel!" is a completely different reaction from, "Can anything good come out of Nazareth?"

Of course, this exchange is only the beginning for Nathanael and Jesus. They doubtless went on to have many more conversations. But in this initial encounter Jesus could see that Nathanael's instinctive perception had changed, and so John tells us in 1:50: "Jesus answered, 'Do you believe because I told you that I saw you under the fig tree? You will see greater things than these.'"

We see both a beautiful and instructive evolution in our passage, from an instinctive, blind prejudice—"Can anything good come out of Nazareth?"—to, "Rabbi, you are the Son of God! You are the King of Israel!" Again, in the words of D. Moody Smith: *Only being with Jesus provides sufficient basis to understand who he is.* And not just Jesus. Amen.

---

1. D. Moody Smith, "John." *Harper's Bible Commentary.* James L. Mays, General Editor (San Francisco: Harper & Row, Publishers, 1998), 1049.

3
THE RHYTHM OF HABIT

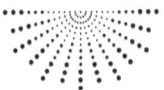

MARK 1:14–20 • 24 JANUARY 2021
THIRD SUNDAY AFTER THE EPIPHANY

¹⁴Now after John was arrested, Jesus came to Galilee, proclaiming the good news of God, ¹⁵and saying, "The time is fulfilled, and the kingdom of God has come near; repent, and believe in the good news." ¹⁶As Jesus passed along the Sea of Galilee, he saw Simon and his brother Andrew casting a net into the sea—for they were fishermen. ¹⁷And Jesus said to them, "Follow me and I will make you fish for people." ¹⁸And immediately they left their nets and followed him. ¹⁹As he went a little farther, he saw James son of Zebedee and his brother John, who were in their boat mending the nets. ²⁰Immediately he called them; and they left their father Zebedee in the boat with the hired men, and followed him.

∽

This past Advent season, I came across a phrase that has made a strong and lasting impression on me: "the rhythm of habit." During the biblical era, commercial fishing was a prosperous business in the Holy Land. Demand was high, and at that time fish were plentiful in the Sea of Galilee. In our own day, we are familiar with family businesses which have been passed down from generation to generation. In the biblical era a family business could be handed down not just for generations, but for centuries. And thus Peter and Andrew and James and John doubtless knew their fishing. In all likelihood their families had been in the business for generations. And thus Peter and Andrew and James and John surely knew *the rhythm of habit*. Commercial fishing was hard work, but profitable. It was what Peter and Andrew and James and John knew. These professional fishermen would have known all about the rhythm of habit.

And then one day a young rabbi approaches. Doubtless he is charismatic. Mark cuts to the chase as he portrays Jesus announcing: "The time is fulfilled, and the kingdom of God has come near; repent, and believe in the good news." And then to Peter and Andrew, in the midst of their familiar routine, Jesus says: "Follow me and I will make you fish for people." This stark invitation calls for a definite response. *Are you coming with me or not? Will you follow me or not?* And, of course, we know their answer: *Yes*. Peter and Andrew, and then James and John answer the call: Follow me... And thus begins the Jesus Movement.

We too are part of the Jesus Movement, the same Jesus Movement whose birth we see portrayed in Mark 1:14–20. Of course, Peter and Andrew and James and John were already people of faith, else they likely would not have been interested in nor moved by what a young rabbi had to say. In commenting on our passage N. T. Wright observes: "Jesus was now calling them to trust the good news that their God was doing something new."[1] Their God *was* doing something new, and Jesus invites these four fishermen to leave their nets and be a part of the movement. *Follow me and I will make you fish for people.*

Jesus did not call these sets of brothers to a spiritual retreat. The movement did not seek to wall itself off from the rest of the world. The movement was *for* the world. "The time is fulfilled, and *the kingdom of God* (emphasis added) has come near; repent, and believe in the good news." The message, the movement, was for all, and Jesus knew that it would take people like Peter and Andrew and James and John—people like us—to spread the good news of the inbreaking of the kingdom.

We are all out of our routines, we are out of our 'rhythm' because of the pandemic. As individuals, as a parish church—and as a nation—we are all out of our rhythm. So much that is familiar and comfortable to us has been turned on its head beginning last March. Due to the pandemic, churches, for the first time, went to online worship out of necessity. We all know the truism: Necessity is the mother of invention. There have been grievous losses during the pandemic, including the familiarity, the rhythm, the habit of regular contact with friends and family. Regarding our parish in particular, we have lost many opportunities for fellowship. And yet, we started to notice something as online worship found its footing. In the Comments section we began to see the names of people unfamiliar to us, some of them from this area, and others from places far and wide. We also noticed people beginning to reconnect with St. Luke's; parishioners who moved away years ago or had lost touch with us one way or another can now reconnect with us digitally. As online worship gained an audience we began to realize that the 'footprint' of St. Luke's was growing larger than ever.

I can remember going over to my office after church on a particular Sunday and checking the Comments section. Someone near to us geographically but new to the church said: "I'm less than a mile from you." *Less than a mile*. The very next comment stated: "We're checking in from Costa Rica." Ironically, in the midst of an ongoing pandemic our 'mission field' has opened up. In this new era of digital connection we realize that there are now few inherent geographic boundaries that limit the reach of this or any other church. Early on in the pandemic I read an article online in which an author in the UK stated: Every Sunday morning I now can choose whether I want to go to church in Bristol or Oxford or Salisbury or London. Increasingly, people near and far are learning that they now can choose to worship with *us*.

There have been some awful disruptions to our rhythms of habit during the pandemic, and yet at the same time a whole new world of possibilities has opened to us. And in terms of the Church at large, local congregations now have opportunities to share the Gospel of Jesus Christ with more people than ever before. *Follow me and I will make you fish for people.* For us that used to mean primarily Cleveland, Bradley County, and the surrounding area. But now it means the entire region, the nation, and yes, even the world. In less than a year, our mission field has expanded in ways that none of us had ever thought to imagine.

"The time is fulfilled, and the kingdom of God has come near; repent, and believe in the good news." None of us would have chosen the disruptions to our routines that we have been experiencing for nearly a year. No sane person would choose for this pandemic to impact the entire world with so much pain, so much uncertainty, so much loss. And yet... As is so often the case, this crisis does bring with it opportunities: opportunities for us to rethink, to reimagine, and to reprioritize what really matters— even what is possible. Just think about the once seemingly limitless possibilities now squarely before us.

It must have been a startling and disrupting invitation to those fishermen on what had started out to be a seemingly ordinary day: "Follow me and I will make you fish for people." The same invitation is now issued to us in this season which brings with it both crisis and opportunity: *Follow me...* Amen.

---

1. N. T. Wright, *Mark for Everyone* (London: Society for Promoting Christian Knowledge, 2001), 10.

4
THUNDERSTRUCK

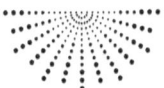

MARK 1:21-28 • 4 FEBRUARY 2021
FOURTH SUNDAY AFTER THE EPIPHANY

²¹They went to Capernaum; and when the sabbath came, he entered the synagogue and taught. ²²They were astounded at his teaching, for he taught them as one having authority, and not as the scribes. ²³Just then there was in their synagogue a man with an unclean spirit, ²⁴and he cried out, "What have you to do with us, Jesus of Nazareth? Have you come to destroy us? I know who you are, the Holy One of God." ²⁵But Jesus rebuked him, saying, "Be silent, and come out of him!" ²⁶And the unclean spirit, convulsing him and crying with a loud voice, came out of him. ²⁷They were all amazed, and they kept on asking one another, "What is this? A new teaching —with authority! He commands even the unclean spirits, and they obey him." ²⁸At once his fame began to spread throughout the surrounding region of Galilee.

∼

There is scholarly consensus that Mark is the earliest of the four Gospels. Scholarly consensus is hard to come by, but the vast majority of biblical scholars think that Mark is the earliest of the four Gospels. If Mark is indeed the earliest, then he invented the Gospel genre.

Mark 1:1: "The beginning of the good news of Jesus Christ..." The *euangeliou*, the *Gospel* of Jesus Christ. In pioneering the Gospel genre, Mark wrote a kind of biography of Jesus. The Gospels are, in part, biographies. But they are more than that. In the New Testament there is a Greek word—*kerygma*—a noun meaning preaching, proclamation. But *kerygma* does not suggest merely the act of preaching. *Kerygma* has as much or more to do with the content—the message—of the Gospel. To be sure, the Gospels tell us *what* Jesus said and did. But they also tell us *who* Jesus was and is. The Gospels are, in part, biographies of Jesus. But they are more than biographies. The Gospels are *kerygmatic*, proclaiming the Church's foundational message: Jesus is Lord.

We know for sure that Mark is the briefest of the four Gospels. In Mark the action moves at a quick pace. His is an action book. If you pick up any commentary on Mark, *any* commentary, one of the first things noted is Mark's frequent use of the Greek word *euthus*, "immediately." In reading through the Gospel of Mark we experience the narrative consistently moving forward at a rapid pace. An action Gospel indeed.

Mark does not offer his readers a birth narrative. Instead, he launches right into his story of Jesus' adult life and ministry. Our passage is taken from chapter one, and Jesus' public ministry has already begun. And much of that public ministry takes place in synagogues. A synagogue functioned as what we would call a church. But synagogues were more than that. They functioned as community centers. Education was offered in the local synagogue. The synagogue was the social nexus of the village. People gathered at the synagogue for much more than worship. So that is where Jesus went. Jesus met the people where they were, and for the Sabbath he would secure permission from the local leadership to speak in the synagogue.

Mark 1:21–22: "They went to Capernaum; and when the sabbath came, he entered the synagogue and taught. They were astounded at his teaching, for he taught them as one having authority, and not as the scribes." In the biblical era, scribes were not primarily copyists in the sense that we might use the term. They were instead experts on Jewish law. Scribes understood their mission largely in terms of passing on the Tradition. Contrary to the scribes, Jesus spoke and acted from the perspective of a more intimate relationship with God and thus exercised more freedom in his interpretation of the law.

Ralph Martin comments on 1:21–22: "[Jesus] began to teach with *firsthand* (emphasis added) authority…"[1] As we might expect, Mark's account is brief, and he does not actually tell us what Jesus said that day in the synagogue. But we know in part what he did: he performed an exorcism, and the people in the synagogue saw firsthand Jesus' power. Mark tells us that they were asking: "What is this? A new teaching—with authority!" Jesus was not simply passing on the Tradition; he was offering his hearers a new, a fresh interpretation—a firsthand experience of God's love and grace.

And for those who followed Jesus with devotion, he generated trust. People saw Jesus' charisma. They saw his power. They heard him preach like no one else had ever preached and teach like no one else had ever taught, and so those who followed Jesus did so from a place of deep trust. In his commentary on our passage, N. T. Wright states: "Without trust breaking through afresh we condemn ourselves to bleak, cynical lives."[2] As the pandemic grinds on, and in this cultural moment when partisanship runs so deep that the very fabric of our nation is under strain, we are wise to think about the place of trust in our lives. Who? What? When? How can we trust in this season filled with so much anxiety? Without trust breaking through afresh, we do indeed condemn ourselves to bleak, cynical lives. Wright's observation was first offered in 2001, over 20 years ago. And yet, think how insightful his words are for the moment that is now.

In the midst of so many uncertainties, we need an anchor. In times like this we need to be sure of our guiding principles. We gather for worship to remind ourselves that we do have an anchor; we do have a set of abidingly instructive guiding principles. We have been shown what it looks like to love and to trust. We have been shown what it looks like to forgive and to seek reconciliation. We have been shown the love of Jesus Christ. *He* is our anchor.

The pandemic has been going on long enough that analysts are already studying its effect on culture. Just this past week I saw a survey indicating the significant uptick in our country in people's interest in spirituality. The survey notes that many are considering afresh the place of spirituality in their lives. We are in one of those moments in our culture when people are stepping back from the trees to see the forest. This is a time for us all to rethink what is most important, most dear to us. And it is especially important for churches to be aware of what is happening in our culture—this uptick in interest in spirituality. This is a time for our local church, and for all churches, to look beyond the 'four walls' and see people who are hungry for trustworthy news of love and hope. *Without trust breaking through afresh, we condemn ourselves to bleak, cynical lives.*

The author of the Gospel of Mark was inspired to craft a new genre of literature. No one before had ever written a Gospel. What people had up to that point were oral traditions, and perhaps a written compilation of some of Jesus' teachings. It was Mark who had the inspiration to craft a narrative, the *kerygma*. Mark pioneered a genre—he wrote a Gospel—in order to proclaim: We can trust both the man Jesus and his message.

"They were astounded at his teaching, for he taught them as one having authority, and not as the scribes." Most translations go with "astounded" here. Others go with "astonished." It has been suggested that we can think of "astounded" here as "they were thunderstruck" by the authority, and the authenticity with which Jesus taught and acted. The New Jerusalem Bible translates the verse: "And his teaching made a deep impression on them because, unlike the scribes, he taught them with authority." I appreciate these nuanced differences in translation. He made a "deep impression." People understood, and they trusted. They could feel the closeness Jesus shared with the Spirit of Divine Love. Without trust breaking through afresh...

This is a moment for us all to allow a fresh, renewed, and hopeful sense of the presence of Christ into our lives. We are all tired of the pandemic. We are tired of the uncertainties. We are tired of the pain and the dislocations. Simultaneously, we are experiencing so much stark, inherently divisive and seemingly intractable partisanship in our culture. It is as if, in holding different points of view, we become enemies of each other. Of all times, this is a moment for a fresh sense of trust to come to us.

About three weeks ago I stood in this spot officiating the Thursday 12:10 p.m. service. At the appointed time, I got up to read the Gospel lesson for the day and to give a brief homily. Suddenly I realized that I did not have my glasses. Until relatively recently that would not have made a big difference, but these days I cannot read anything up close without my glasses. So I stood *here* in this very spot to read the Gospel lesson and to preach and realized: *I don't have my glasses on!* And as I did the best I could with the blurred lines I wondered where I had left my glasses—on my desk or in the sacristy or in my pants pocket?—all the while asking myself: *How could I have forgotten my glasses?* And then, just as suddenly, I realized that I did in fact have them. Without my realizing it they had slid down my nose, and I was looking *over* them instead of *through* them. Not my finest moment. And yet... When I realized that I did have my glasses on and repositioned them, suddenly everything came into focus. In an instant, I could see with clarity.

We are in a cultural moment when it is crucial for us to focus in on the ways and wisdom of Jesus Christ. In a moment when there is so much anxiety, so much pain, so many uncertainties, it is crucially important for us to hear afresh the message of the Gospel. Mark, Matthew, Luke and John have left us a wonderful legacy—the Gospel genre. They have given us everything we need to find the Good News. Amen.

---

1. Ralph P. Martin, *Mark*. Knox Preaching Guides. John H. Hayes, Editor (Atlanta: John Knox Press, 1981), 14.
2. N. T. Wright, *Twelve Months of Sundays: Biblical Meditations on the Christian Years A, B & C* (New York: Morehouse Publishing, 2012), 154.

5
A MIXTURE OF AWE AND TERROR

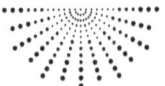

MARK 9:2-9 • 14 FEBRUARY 2021
TRANSFIGURATION SUNDAY
LAST SUNDAY AFTER THE EPIPHANY

²Six days later, Jesus took with him Peter and James and John, and led them up a high mountain apart, by themselves. And he was transfigured before them, ³and his clothes became dazzling white, such as no one on earth could bleach them. ⁴And there appeared to them Elijah with Moses, who were talking with Jesus. ⁵Then Peter said to Jesus, "Rabbi, it is good for us to be here; let us make three dwellings, one for you, one for Moses, and one for Elijah." ⁶He did not know what to say, for they were terrified. ⁷Then a cloud overshadowed them, and from the cloud there came a voice, "This is my Son, the Beloved; listen to him!" ⁸Suddenly when they looked around, they saw no one with them any more, but only Jesus. ⁹As they were coming down the mountain, he ordered them to tell no one about what they had seen, until after the Son of Man had risen from the dead.

If we are fortunate, we have moments in life when everything seems to be just right, and in those rare and precious moments we may think: *If only this moment could last forever.* We are indeed fortunate to have such moments, and we may think of them as 'mountaintop' experiences. We are most fortunate when we are truly at peace and, at least for the moment, all seems well.

Of course, such moments can take many forms. In preparing for this address I was reminded of a number of the concerts I have attended over the years. In the days of my youth, 105 Maple Drive was awash with country music during the week, and Southern Gospel on the weekend. I grew up on a steady diet of country mixed with gospel. But then came my teenage years, and you know what happened: *rock and roll*! Which brings me back to the thought of concerts. I have been to a lot of great shows in my day. Those of us who have been to rock concerts remember those times when the band has just finished their 'final' song and are exiting the stage. The arena goes dark. Then what happens? The applause, which had momentarily waned, starts to rebuild. Back in the day we would hold up our lighters with the flame ignited. Now, of course, people use their phones. With time the roar of the crowd gets louder and louder. We want more. We want an encore. And on a good night, one by one, the band members come back out, and the lights come back up, and the roar gets even louder. Why? Because it is not over after all. The concert is not finished. There *is* more. But not for long. And then it really is over.

Of course, the music has to stop at some point. At some point we all have to come down from the 'mountaintop' of an exhilarating show. Those of us of a certain age will know how to complete this sentence: Ladies and gentlemen, *Elvis has left the building.*

Fleming Rutledge is one of the preachers I most admire. In a sermon on the Transfiguration she writes: "It is part of our fallen human nature to want to build booths and ski lodges and resort hotels on top of mountains. We don't want to come down from the high."[1] Surely most if not all of us can remember those times when we were on a mountaintop, or at the beach, and thought, *If only...*

The Transfiguration is a pivotal moment in the life and ministry of Jesus. And what the inner circle of his disciples experienced in that moment must have been a mixture of awe-inspiring and terrifying, given the depth of the holiness of what was happening right before their eyes. In the Transfiguration the 'veil' was lifted, the 'curtain' was pulled back, and in that moment of holiness the gap between heaven and earth was bridged. And so it makes perfect sense for Peter to have said: "Rabbi, it is good for us to be here..." It makes all the sense in the world to want to preserve such an unimaginably holy experience—a true moment of transcendence. And so Peter thinks impulsively and practically. Who can blame him for wanting to preserve this mountaintop experience? It *is* part of our fallen human nature to want to build 'ski lodges' and 'resort hotels' on top of mountains. We *do not* want to come down from the high.

And then Mark 9:8 leads into 9:9: "As they were coming down the mountain..." Jesus knew that his ministry was not yet finished. He knew that his work was not yet done. In the aforementioned sermon on the Transfiguration Rutledge observes: "On this day, Jesus turns his back on his glory and begins his descent into the valley."[2]

Worship is meant to be a mountaintop experience. To be sure, some weeks we feel it more than others, but liturgy is meant to offer a 'moment' when the gap between heaven and earth is bridged. In the Orthodox tradition, Divine Liturgy is framed as offering worshippers a foretaste of heaven. In reality, for all Christians, liturgy—worship—is meant to be understood and experienced as a foretaste of heaven. Every worship service, however seemingly modest, or 'normal,' is meant to be a kind of mountaintop moment through which we are drawn at least a little closer to the love and peace of God.

Christians are meant to gather regularly to talk of spirituality.

And it is essential that we do so. We must 'talk the talk': hear and reflect upon the Scriptures and pray together in the context of worship. Then there comes that moment when the worship service ends, and then it is time to 'walk the walk.' The 'talk' of worship is essential. It is foundational to the Christian life. These oftentimes modest 'mountaintop' experiences of regular worship help to keep us on track spiritually. But then, inexorably, we are called back into the 'valley' of everyday living, taking Jesus Christ and his love with us back into the routine of our daily lives. We love the mountaintop, and rightly so, but the vast majority of our lives are spent in the valley.

Here is another quotation from Fleming Rutledge's Transfiguration Sunday sermon titled: "The Love Olympics Go to Jerusalem."

> A few years back, I was crossing the street near my parish in New York City. A taxi came roaring around the corner and knocked me to the pavement. A crowd gathered, and an ambulance was called. It took an unusually long time to arrive. It was forty minutes before I was actually put on the gurney. In the meantime, I lay on the asphalt. I was aware of a lot of people standing around looking down at me. What I remember most about that long wait was the great distance between me on the concrete and the faces high above. In those minutes I very much needed someone to get down on the ground with me, to put a coat under my head, to hold my hand and *stay down* with me until help arrived.[3]

What a poignant reflection on a valley moment. Fleming Rutledge, one of the great preachers of our time, flat on her back, just wanting someone, *anyone,* to kneel down and be with her in her moment of need.

We are now approaching the one-year mark of the pandemic. Like all of you, I too am getting so weary of all this. Seriously! But as the pandemic grinds on, I do allow myself to picture the nave once again full on Sundays. Occasionally I even allow myself to imagine the sound of folding chairs being deployed at the last minute like we sometimes have had to do at the late service in years past, in 'normal' times. There are times when I imagine the sound of the choir singing. And I allow myself to imagine the Parish House on a normal Sunday morning, with doors slamming, and children laughing, and me hearing that occasional "Fr. Joel!" that I love and miss so much, Surely we all allow ourselves in our minds to hear the sounds of children and youth back with us enjoying being reunited with their church friends. And we *will* get there. But in the meantime we still have our work to do. The service of others, yes, but also the work of personal transformation. In this season of global pandemic *and* intense social stirring, if we will open up our eyes, our minds—our hearts—we can decide to see this time that none of us would have chosen as a wake-up call. We can redeem this time in the valley by reexamining and reprioritizing what matters most to us as modern-day disciples of Jesus.

None of us would have chosen this season in the valley, this wilderness time. And yet...This time of trial can be redeemed, and we can emerge from this season of pandemic *and* racial reckoning transformed. Renewed. Humbler. More compassionate. More teachable. More aware than ever before of the importance, indeed, the imperative, of our calling as followers of Jesus Christ.

The Transfiguration was truly one of the pivotal moments in the life and ministry of Jesus. In that profoundly holy moment he was revealed to be the very image, the very embodiment, of the Son of God. And in that extraordinary moment his closest friends were right to realize: *This is not just another rabbi. We are witnessing in him holiness the likes of which we have never seen.* And thus it made perfect sense for them to want to extend the moment, to preserve it indefinitely. But Jesus knew that as important as the mountaintop is, the vast majority of his—and our—life's work takes place in the valley.

I will never forget the moment when I saw a picture of a

particular church's interior. Over the door through which the people in that church leave week after week to go back into the world they see painted in a beautiful yet simple script: "OUR WORSHIP HAS ENDED. NOW OUR SERVICE BEGINS." Amen.

---

1. Fleming Rutledge, *The Bible and the New York Times.* Paperback edition (Grand Rapids: William B. Eerdmans Publishing Company,1999), 83.
2. *Ibid.*, 85.
3. *Ibid.*, 83.

6
THE UNMISTAKABLE VOICE THAT MATTERS

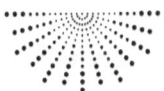

MARK 1:9–15 • 21 FEBRUARY 2021
FIRST SUNDAY IN LENT

⁹In those days Jesus came from Nazareth of Galilee and was baptized by John in the Jordan. ¹⁰And just as he was coming up out of the water, he saw the heavens torn apart and the Spirit descending like a dove on him. ¹¹And a voice came from heaven, "You are my Son, the Beloved; with you I am well pleased." ¹²And the Spirit immediately drove him out into the wilderness. ¹³He was in the wilderness forty days, tempted by Satan; and he was with the wild beasts; and the angels waited on him. ¹⁴Now after John was arrested, Jesus came to Galilee, proclaiming the good news of God, ¹⁵and saying, "The time is fulfilled, and the kingdom of God has come near; repent, and believe in the good news."

∽

In commenting on Mark 1:11, Kent Hughes writes: "See and hear the beauty of the moment."[1] "And a voice came from heaven, 'You are my Son, the Beloved; with you I am well pleased.'" Who among us does not long to hear such an expression of pure, unconditional love? Surely we all long to hear: *You are my Beloved.* It is wise counsel from Kent Hughes: See and hear the beauty of the moment.

In his commentary on 1:11, N. T. Wright observes: "The whole Christian gospel could be summed up in this point: that when the living God looks at us, at every baptized and believing Christian, he says to us what he said to Jesus on that day. He sees us, not as we are in ourselves, but as we are in Jesus Christ."[2] A strong statement. The whole Christian gospel *can* be summed up in this point, coming to understand that in Jesus we also are the Beloved of God. Many of us may think instinctively that Christianity is primarily about selflessness, servanthood, sacrificing for the good of others—all in the name of Jesus Christ. And at one level this is true. Christianity *is* about selflessness, servanthood, and sacrificing for the good of others—but from whence? Our desire to be selfless, our will to serve is meant to come from a place of gratitude—gratitude for God's love for us, made known to us most fully in Jesus. The writer says it so beautifully and movingly in 1 John 4:11: "Beloved, since God loved us so much, we also ought to love one another." And just eight verses later in 4:19: "We love [him] because he first loved us."

One of the great preachers of our time is Mark Oakley, dean of St. John's College, Cambridge. He has an article about Lent in this week's issue of *Church Times* titled: "A Battle for the Heart." In the article, Oakley observes that oftentimes we are two things at once. We are saint *and* sinner. We are good *and* bad. We are selfless *and* selfish. There is a battle for the heart going on all the time. The battle for the heart goes back and forth, on and on, all our days.

In commenting on 1:11, Oakley writes: "Coming up out of the water, [Jesus] had heard the unmistakable voice that matters, telling him he was cherished, wanted, and ready."[3] *The unmistakable voice that matters.* The voice of Truth. The voice of Divine Love. The voice we know we are meant to follow.

One way for us to frame this new season of Lent might be to recognize that it is a season to remember to listen for the unmistakable voice that matters. Lent is meant to be a season during which we are particularly intentional in listening for the voice we know to be true, that steadily consistent voice of love and grace. They are beautiful words, are they not? *You are my Beloved.*

The very first prayer of the Ash Wednesday liturgy begins: "Almighty and everlasting God, you hate nothing you have made and forgive the sins of all who are penitent..."[4] It is important for us to remember that the opening prayer of the season of Lent strikes an unmistakable note of grace. Lord, you *do not* hate anything you have made. You do not hate *anyone* you have made, and you forgive *all* who are penitent. Echoes of that unmistakable, trustworthy, omnipresent voice of grace, if we will but hear it. *You are my Beloved.*

Some of the best pastoral advice I have ever heard is: "Preach grace, and keep the service to an hour." Fantastic pastoral wisdom. Preach grace—always. Preach grace every chance you get, *and* keep the service to an hour! In a moment of, yes—amazing grace —Jesus comes up out of the water and hears: *You are my Son, the Beloved; with you I am well pleased.*

Our passage is set in the context of Jesus' baptism, which puts us in mind of our own baptismal liturgy. In this church, immediately following the act of baptism the priest calls the baptized by name and says: "you are sealed by the Holy Spirit in Baptism and marked as Christ's own for ever."[5] Notice, that statement does not include the words until, unless, or except. The statement is unambiguous. You *are* sealed by the Holy Spirit in Baptism and marked as Christ's own for ever. A moment of grace: amazing grace.

I had reason this past week to pay a brief visit to our memorial garden, and among several names on the wall that caught my eye was that of Bobbie Crook, a long-time and much beloved member of this church. Bobbie had a wonderful sense of humor. She was simply one of *the* funniest human beings I have ever met. And she had a servant's heart. She would do anything for anyone whom she could help. Toward the end of her life Bobbie fought an especially courageous battle with cancer. She lived much longer, and with more quality of life than any of her doctors expected. But she was sick for a long time, and in those days I would visit her regularly and take communion to her. Near the end, when she knew her days really were numbered, as one particular visit was coming to an end, Bobbie looked at me and said: "Joel, you are a beautiful person." I can remember that moment as if it were yesterday. Completely unbidden: "Joel, you are a beautiful person." And in that moment my instinctive reaction, which I reflexively verbalized to her, was: "No, I'm not." Subtextually, I was thinking: I'm not as good as you think I am. I'm not always this sweet. I'm not always this kind. It was an instinctive, reflexive, and, in the moment, an involuntary verbal response: "No, I'm not." Bobbie then looked at me with a mixture of sweetness, conviction, and correction(!) and said: "Yes, you are."

I can remember that exchange as if it had happened yesterday. In the immediate aftermath of that visit, as I thought about what she had said to me I realized in a deeper way than ever before that my predisposition, my default setting, is one of guilt. My default setting *is* one of guilt, but on that memorable day Bobbie was offering me the alternative of grace. Unbidden, unexpected, and, to my mind, undeserved. And yet, at Bobbie's urging, gratefully received. Bobbie knew that her days, and so our visits, were numbered, and in that moment she chose to offer me a word of grace. From earlier in today's liturgy: "Water, river, spirit, grace, sweep over me, sweep over me!"[6]

We are the Beloved. From our gracious Lord we have been given the greatest gift that we can ever receive—absolute, unconditional pardon for our inevitable human selfishness. And thus our predisposition *can be* one of peace instead of guilt. And in that sense, this *is* what the Gospel is all about. When we boil it down, what is the Good News? That we are offered radical welcome and spiritual communion, not just with each other, but with our Divine Source, who gives us life and breath. We do not have to be weighed down by a predisposition of guilt. If and when we choose, our fundamental orientation can be that of claiming our Belovedness in the eyes of God.

Today is the First Sunday in Lent. When we think of the season of Lent we may think of it as an annual season of reflection, of introspection, and—using a word essential to the season of Lent—repentance. Repentance in the New Testament has a very straightforward definition. It means a change of mind: "*repent* (emphasis added), and believe in the good news." A change of mind can be subtle. It can happen quietly. But every day of our lives, during Lent or not, the message of the Gospel is: Turn from the weight of guilt and relish the freedom of grace. You *are* the Beloved of God.

I was in my home study this past Wednesday afternoon between the noon and the 6:00 p.m. Ash Wednesday services preparing for the Lenten series which begins on Tuesday night. I was consulting several of the books in my library on the Gospel of Mark: some of them big, thick books. As I was putting one of those books back after I had finished with it and was reaching for another, a little, tiny book, very nearly the smallest book I own, fell from the shelf. That tiny little paperback fell from the shelf and landed at my feet. Once it landed, all there was to do was to reach down and pick it up. Keep in mind, this is all happening on *Ash Wednesday*.

As it turned out, the book in question is one of my favorite little devotional books, *A Common Prayer*, by Michael Leunig. The book is filled with brief, one-page meditations alongside some wonderfully simple yet deeply evocative illustrations. On Ash Wednesday(!), as I was working dutifully and diligently preparing for my upcoming Lenten series, *A Common Prayer* fell from the shelf, landed at my feet, and fell open to one of my favorite passages in the book which I had not thought about in months. But of all days, on Ash Wednesday, the passage was *given* to me, and now, on this First Sunday in Lent, I give it to you.

There are only two feelings. Love and fear. There are only two languages. Love and fear. There are only two activities. Love and fear. There are only two motives, two procedures, two frameworks, two results. Love and fear. Love and fear.[7]

Amen.

---

1. R. Kent Hughes, *Mark: Jesus, Servant and Savior.* Preaching the Word. R. Kent Hughes, Editor (Wheaton, IL: Crossway, 2015), 24.
2. N. T. Wright, *Mark for Everyone* (London: Society for Promoting Christian Knowledge, 2001), 4.
3. Mark Oakley, "A Battle for the Heart." *Church Times*, 12 February 2021. https://www.churchtimes.co.uk/articles/2021/12-february/faith/faith-features/a-battle-for-the-heart
4. *The Book of Common Prayer* (New York: The Seabury Press, 1979), 264.
5. *Ibid.*, 308.
6. Michael Leunig. *A Common Prayer* (North Blackburn, Victoria, Australia: Collins Dove Publishers, 1990), unnumbered page.
7. *Ibid.*

7
IN THE LIGHT OF EASTER

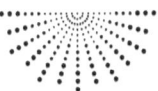

MARK 8:31–38 • 28 FEBRUARY 2021
SECOND SUNDAY IN LENT

³¹Jesus began to teach them that the Son of Man must undergo great suffering, and be rejected by the elders, the chief priests, and the scribes, and be killed, and after three days rise again. ³²He said all this quite openly. And Peter took him aside and began to rebuke him. ³³But turning and looking at his disciples, he rebuked Peter and said, "Get behind me, Satan! For you are setting your mind not on divine things but on human things." ³⁴He called the crowd with his disciples, and said to them, "If any want to become my followers, let them deny themselves and take up their cross and follow me. ³⁵For those who want to save their life will lose it, and those who lose their life for my sake, and for the sake of the gospel, will save it. ³⁶For what will it profit them to gain the whole world and forfeit their life? ³⁷Indeed, what can they give in return for their life? ³⁸Those who are ashamed of me and of my words in this adulterous and sinful generation, of them the Son of Man will also be ashamed when he comes in the glory of his Father with the holy angels."

To get the full import of Mark 8:31–38, it is important to place it in its literary context by also reading Mark 8:27–30.

> ²⁷Jesus went on with his disciples to the villages of Caesarea Philippi; and on the way he asked his disciples, "Who do people say that I am?" ²⁸And they answered him, "John the Baptist; and others, Elijah; and still others, one of the prophets." ²⁹He asked them, "But who do you say that I am?" Peter answered him, "You are the Messiah." ³⁰And he sternly ordered them not to tell anyone about him."

We are at a pivotal point in Mark's story of Jesus. Christians gather for worship week after week to affirm our belief that Jesus is the Christ, the Son of God, and we do so with the benefit of 2,000 years of Christian history and theology at our disposal. Christianity has had two millennia to reflect on who Jesus was and is. But the disciples experienced Jesus' life and ministry in real time, without the benefit of hindsight. And thus it is a monumental moment when Peter says on behalf of the disciples: "You are the Messiah."

In order to make the most sense of 8:31–38 we have to take on board the full weight of what Peter has just affirmed. In following Jesus, the disciples have risked everything. They have given up their lives as they knew them in order to follow this young rabbi whom they have come to believe is the Anointed One of God. And so it was a watershed moment, and in the moment, Peter must have expected praise for giving the right answer: *You are the Messiah*. But Jesus seized upon it as primarily a teachable moment.

Mark 8:31: "Then he began to teach them that the Son of Man must undergo great suffering, and be rejected by the elders, the chief priests, and the scribes, and be killed, and after three days rise again." This is not what the disciples would have expected to hear! For them, to think of Jesus being the Messiah would have brought with it a connotation of triumph and future glory for

Jesus and for themselves. They would have thought of their close relationship with Jesus in terms of his increasing earthly acclaim and his future political power—and theirs. But Jesus uses this teachable moment to instruct them that *his* vision involves humility and sacrifice—then vindication and ultimately glory.

Jesus' teaching about humility, suffering, and death, plus his mysterious talk of rising again, would have stopped the disciples in their tracks. It is Peter who has the nerve to speak on behalf of the group in protest. There was nothing in Jewish theology that would have provided the intellectual framework for Jews to understand that the Messiah would be betrayed by his own people and suffer death at the hands of a hated foreign power. Nothing in their background would have helped the disciples make sense of what Jesus was telling them.

Jesus responds to Peter's rebuke: "Get behind me, Satan! For you are setting your mind not on divine things but on human things." This is a moment of high drama, and of lasting import. *You are the Messiah* would have marked a spiritual highpoint for the disciples, but Jesus grasps the importance of the moment to teach them *his* vocational understanding. And when Peter rebukes him, Jesus does not hesitate to stand his ground.

Kent Hughes writes in his commentary on our passage: "These were the harshest words Jesus ever spoke to a devoted, well-meaning heart!"[1] A strong statement. Clearly, Peter *is* devoted. He has put his life on hold in order to follow Jesus. There is a similarly strong rebuke elsewhere in the Gospels. In Matthew 4:1–11, the devil tempts Jesus to reject the call on his life, and it is in 4:10 that we read Jesus' rebuke of the tempter: "Away with you, Satan! for it is written, 'Worship the Lord your God, and serve only him.'" But our passage does contain the harshest words Jesus ever spoke to a *devoted, well-meaning heart*. Just imagine how shocking it must have been for Peter to be rebuked so strongly by the one in whom he had placed his entire faith. None of us like to be in the position of being embarrassed or humiliated in front of our friends. In time, the disciples would come to understand Jesus' teaching. In the light of Easter, everything that Jesus had said regarding his dying and rising would eventually make sense to them. But in the moment, Peter dared to speak his mind, and in doing so he walked right into a teachable moment. Doubtless he was stung. It had to hurt Peter deeply to hear such strong, corrective language from the man he loved and respected more than anyone else.

The English priest and spiritual writer Michael Mayne often observed: "Life has a way of reducing us to our proper size." There is a lot of truth in that. A one-liner full of insight: *Life has a way of reducing us to our proper size.* We have all been there. We know what it is like when a rebuke, a harsh and cutting remark really stings and hurts us—stops us in our tracks. We all know what it is like to get out of line, to get out of our lane, and to say or do the wrong thing. When we are honest with ourselves, surely we can all relate to Peter. In his defense, he had given the right answer! *You are the Christ.* But he thought this meant Jesus' eventual rise to power as an earthly king reminiscent of the great King David. But Jesus seizes the moment to teach not only Peter but all the disciples that his is a different vision, that he has come not to lord political power over people, but to serve them, to embody and demonstrate the depths of God's love and grace. In the moment, Peter must have been deeply hurt and embarrassed, even angry. But his harsh rebuke of Peter notwithstanding, Jesus' love for him never wavers. Jesus never gives up on him. Every time Peter makes a mistake, Jesus is willing and ready to forgive. Here I am reminded of the Benedictine motto: "Always we begin again."

Whenever I think of Peter and his missteps I am reminded of an ancient exhortation that comes to us from Japanese culture: "Fall down seven times, stand up eight." Such a hauntingly crisp and clear teaching: *Fall down seven times, stand up eight.* This venerable Eastern wisdom complements well the Gospel message of forgiveness and grace. Peter's mistakes are always met with forgiveness and the offer of a new, a fresh start. *Always we begin again.*

In addition to, "Life has a way of reducing us to our proper size," Michael Mayne was also fond of another truism which is especially apt for both Mark 8:31–38 and this Second Sunday in Lent. "God's judgment is always more than matched by his mercy." Amen.

---

1. R. Kent Hughes, *Mark: Jesus, Servant and Savior.* Preaching the Word. R. Kent Hughes, Editor (Wheaton, IL: Crossway, 2015), 197.

8

A TRUTH THAT TRANSCENDS THE PANDEMIC

JOHN 3:14–21 • 14 MARCH 2021
FOURTH SUNDAY IN LENT

¹⁴Jesus said, "And just as Moses lifted up the serpent in the wilderness, so must the Son of Man be lifted up, ¹⁵that whoever believes in him may have eternal life. ¹⁶For God so loved the world that he gave his only Son, so that everyone who believes in him may not perish but may have eternal life. ¹⁷Indeed, God did not send his Son into the world to condemn the world, but in order that the world might be saved through him. ¹⁸Those who believe in him are not condemned; but those who do not believe are condemned already, because they have not believed in the name of the only Son of God. ¹⁹And this is the judgment, that the light has come into the world, and people loved darkness rather than light because their deeds were evil. ²⁰For all who do evil hate the light and do not come to the light, so that their deeds may not be exposed. ²¹But those who do what is true come to the light, so that it may be clearly seen that their deeds have been done in God."

In his commentary on John 3:14–21 Gerard Sloyan writes regarding 3:16: "For many, the Gospel peaks here."[1] *For God so loved the world that he gave his only Son, so that everyone who believes in him may not perish but may have eternal life.* John 3:16 is surely the most familiar verse in all of the New Testament. That said, what follows is not bad either. We read in 3:17: "Indeed, God did not send the Son into the world to condemn the world, but in order that the world might be saved through him."

This past Friday afternoon, like a lot of you have done, I got my first COVID shot. One year ago today it would have seemed impossible that, in just a year's time, we would have a safe and effective vaccine. Most people said that it was impossible, including most 'experts,' and yet others dreamed, planned, *worked*, and brought a safe and effective vaccine to the public within the span of one year. To be sure, we are still in the grip of the pandemic, and yet there is also reason to hope.

While waiting to get my shot I ran into a friend who was doing the same thing. We had some time to talk, and we both commented that, at long last, it seems as if we are finally turning a corner, that things really are starting to look up. While that may be true, we still must be vigilant. Anyone who has ever been around track and field at any level knows the term: Run through the tape. To run through the tape means not letting up before crossing the finish line. The pandemic is not over; we are not yet out of the woods. And yet... We do have reason to believe that better days are ahead.

This past week we marked the one-year anniversary of the declaration of a global pandemic. A year we cannot forget. A year we dare not forget. One year ago not one of us knew for sure that we would be here today. I live a busy, active, robustly healthy life. And yet... I have comorbidities that do not react well to the COVID virus. A year ago today I did not *know* that I would be here today. If we are honest with ourselves, we all have had that reality come clear to us this past year. And yet... Here we are.

On this first anniversary it is important for us to ask ourselves: What have we learned thus far? And what are the lessons that we are still learning? With what must we still come to terms? It is time for us to acknowledge and wrestle with such questions. And thus what better day could there be to hear John 3:16? *For God so loved the world that he gave his only Son, so that everyone who believes in him may not perish but may have eternal life.*

The Greek for *eternal life* occurs seventeen times in John. The author introduces us to the term "eternal life" here in chapter three, and goes on to employ the term sixteen more times. On the first anniversary of the declaration of a global pandemic, the lectionary has given us one of the most familiar, one of the most instructive, and one of the most reassuring verses in all of Scripture.

As a rising junior in college, I was a history and political science double major with a minor in sociology. At that point, I was not yet even minoring in religion. Going into my junior year I tried to sign up for an upper-level political science seminar called "The President, Congress, and Public Policy." I can remember the exact title of the course to this day. But I was too late. Twelve people had already registered for the twelve spots, and thus I missed the class. Needing more humanities credits, I saw that an upper-level course on the Gospel of John was offered, and I thought: I have been in Baptist Sunday School my whole life. One book ought to be easy! So I signed up for "The Gospel of John." As you might imagine, an upper-level college elective turned out to be a little more involved than Sunday School.

While taking the course, something happened that I did not expect. I found my passion. Up to that point, as a history and political science double major, I was thinking seriously about graduate school in history or political science. I also was thinking seriously about a career in the military. But I could not generate a passion for any of those paths. But then I signed up for that course on the Gospel of John, and I found it—my passion, my 'bliss.' The serious, sustained, intellectually rigorous study of Scripture generated in me a passion that I had yet to discover until 'happening' upon that course on John.

As an undergraduate I learned that in the Fourth Gospel eternal life is understood not only as life after death, but as a dimension or quality of life that is already a present possibility for the person who believes in Jesus. Simply put, *eternal life* in the Gospel of John refers not only to the future, but also to a quality of life offered to us in the present. In the Gospel of John *eternal life* is not just a promise for the future, it is a gift offered to us in the here and now. In John, *eternal life* refers to a *quality* of life. Indeed, the primary connotation of "eternal life" is not future bliss but a *present* quality of life, life in the here and now lived in the power of the Spirit. Seventeen times John records Jesus offering people eternal life—a changed life.

From the early days of the pandemic we have heard: "We're all in this together." We have heard it at different times, in various contexts, from a variety of people. *We're all in this together.* And we are *all* in this together. Every one of us is vulnerable. And every one of us has lost someone, or something, in this last year. Not one of us is immune from the realities of the pandemic. But "We're all in this together" is, at a deeper level, a truth that transcends the pandemic. *We're all in this together* is a theology of life, a theology grounded in our shared humanity. "We're all in this together" is more than a strategy to deal with the pandemic. It is a call to a renewal of our understanding of the privilege that it is to be a member of the human race, the human *family—all* of us created in God's own image. All of us equally loved by Love.

Going forward, we have every reason to hope regarding the pandemic. We *will* get through this. And, as people of faith, we have a high calling going forward. We have a lot of hard work to do as individuals, as church members, as a country, and as a global community, to make the vision of One Human Family—a family of equals—a reality.

We really are all in this together. For God so loved the world... Amen.

---

1. Gerard S. Sloyan, *John*. Interpretation: A Bible Commentary for Teaching and Preaching. James L. Mays, Editor (Atlanta: John Knox Press, 1998), 46.

9
DEEP ROOTS, AND YET...

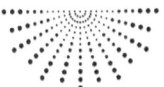

JOHN 12:20–33 • 21 MARCH 2021
FIFTH SUNDAY IN LENT

²⁰Now among those who went up to worship at the festival were some Greeks. ²¹They came to Philip, who was from Bethsaida in Galilee, and said to him, "Sir we wish to see Jesus." ²²Philip went and told Andrew; then Andrew and Philip went and told Jesus. ²³Jesus answered them, "The hour has come for the Son of Man to be glorified. ²⁴Very truly, I tell you, unless a grain of wheat falls into the earth and dies, it remains just a single grain; but if it dies, it bears much fruit. ²⁵Those who love their life lose it, and those who hate their life in this world will keep it for eternal life. ²⁶Whoever serves me must follow me, and where I am, there will my servant be also. Whoever serves me, the Father will honor. ²⁷Now my soul is troubled. And what should I say—'Father, save me from this hour'? No, it is for this reason that I have come to this hour. ²⁸Father, glorify your name." Then a voice came from heaven, "I have glorified it, and I will glorify it again." ²⁹The crowd standing there heard it and said that it was thunder. Others said, "An angel has spoken to him." ³⁰Jesus answered, "This voice has come for your sake, not for mine. ³¹Now is the judgment of this world; now the ruler

of this world will be driven out. ³²And I, when I am lifted up from the earth, will draw all people to myself." ³³He said this to indicate the kind of death he was to die.

∼

Most of us have been fortunate to have had a mentor, or, even better, several mentors. A mentor is defined as: "a trusted counselor or guide: [a] tutor, coach."¹ Think of all those people in your life who have helped to show you the way—those who have encouraged you, believed in you. I have had several mentors, including a junior high school football and baseball coach and a seventh grade World History teacher. In college, graduate school and seminary I was blessed with several professors who were wonderful mentors and remain lastingly significant in my life and ministry. But given my vocation as a parish priest, from a pastoral standpoint, *the* mentor for me was a man named Jim Hindle.

Jim Hindle was the founding priest of a mission church in my hometown in the mid-1950s. My parents remember Fr. Hindle from their high school days. By the time I met Fr. Hindle in the mid-1980s, he was in his maturity and nearing retirement in Bat Cave, North Carolina. People in my hometown still talk about Fr. Hindle and what a faithful priest he was, how open-minded and progressive he was in the 1950s, and that he was well ahead of his time regarding social change. I only got to know Fr. Hindle late in his career, but he was still active and effective in parish ministry even then, and all these years later he remains my role model, my exemplar.

During my senior year of seminary, when it came time for our six-week intensive field education experience I chose to go to Bat Cave, where Fr. Hindle was in his second tenure as rector of Church of the Transfiguration. Most of my classmates went to places like Chicago, Atlanta, or Nashville for their field placements, but I went to Bat Cave(!) because I wanted to do my field education with Fr. Hindle. During those six formative weeks Fr. Hindle taught me three things that I practice to this day.

1. Serve the Lord with gladness (Psalm 100).
2. Do not spend a lot of time solving problems that do not exist.
3. Do not spend a lot of time answering questions that people are not asking.

In John 12:20 we read: "Now among those who went up to worship at the festival [Passover] were some Greeks." "Greeks" here is a catch-all term for Gentiles. These "Greeks" in all likelihood were Gentiles who had an affinity for Judaism but had not yet sought formal entry into the Jewish community. Such persons were known as "God-fearers." We meet several "God-fearers" in the New Testament: the Roman centurion in Luke 7, the Ethiopian court official in Acts 8, and another Roman centurion, Cornelius, in Acts 10.

The Greeks referred to in 12:20 are in Jerusalem for Passover. They seek out Philip (a Greek name) and say: "Sir, we wish to see Jesus." And thus my earlier reference to Fr. Hindle. These Greeks *are* asking the question: May we see Jesus? Doubtless they are also asking: Who is he? And: How is he different from all the other rabbis? What is it that he is teaching and preaching? And, I suspect, as much as anything their question in the end is: Is his message for *us*? Are we Gentiles included in this exceptional rabbi's outreach? These Greeks *are* asking questions. They are clearly interested in learning more about Jesus and his message. They are on a spiritual quest.

Philip did not sit on this. He went and told Andrew (another Greek name) and then Andrew and Philip went and told Jesus. Told him what? That there were some Gentiles present who cared enough to have asked to see him. They cared enough to have sought out Jesus and his disciples.

Jesus responds in 12:23: "The hour has come for the Son of

Man to be glorified." This is a pivotal moment in the life and ministry of Jesus. Heretofore, Jesus' focus has been largely on people within the nation of Israel. Jesus was a Jew, his disciples were Jews, and his ministry started 'at home.' That said, Jesus recognized the approach of these Gentiles as a pivotal moment. The time of fulfillment was at hand. The *universal* scope of Jesus' ministry was about to be made manifest in the events of Good Friday and Easter.

And so John records for us Jesus' words: "The hour has come for the Son of Man to be glorified." This marks a turning point in the Jesus movement. When these Gentiles reach out to Jesus he seizes upon the teachable moment. His message *is* for Gentiles as well as Jews. Earlier in the Gospel of John we read in 3:16: "For God so loved the world..." Not just one nation. Not just one Tradition. For God so loved the *world*...

Our passage concludes with: "'And I, when I am lifted up from the earth, will draw all people to myself.' He said this to indicate the kind of death he was to die." Here we see the shift from Jesus' focus on the nation of Israel to the wider world. And notice the imagery in 12:32: "And I, when I am *lifted up* (emphasis added) from the earth..." In due course Jesus would be nailed to a cross and then 'lifted up' to meet his death. And then would come Easter Day. He was *raised* from the dead. The language here is freighted with meaning. "And I, when I am *lifted up* (emphasis added) from the earth, will draw all people to myself." In this pivotal moment, the scope of Jesus' ministry shifts from being primarily expressed within the nation of Israel to the wider world.

"Sir, we wish to see Jesus." These Gentiles *are* asking questions. Are we included? Is the Good News for us? And Jesus' response is: "The hour has come..."

In commenting on John 12:20–33 and applying it to contemporary life, N. T. Wright observes: "The request to see Jesus may of course be expressed inarticulately or obliquely. We have to learn to hear it within the symbols of a culture as well as in face-to-face questions."[2] An insightful observation. Spiritual hunger need not be expressed necessarily in specifically religious language. People may well be hungry for a deeper experience of God's love but may not express that desire in traditional religious language, or may not be looking for a response couched in traditional religious terms. Wright is nonetheless encouraging us to be able to hear and pick up on spiritual hunger people may make known to us in any number of ways. And it is incumbent upon us to understand in our contemporary culture that an interest in spirituality may not always be expressed in terms of church attendance. People may well be interested in spirituality without thinking or speaking in specifically traditional religious language. But just because their wording is not traditional does not mean that their interest is not there. It does not mean that the questions are not being asked, however indirectly: What is it that your church believes? How is it that your church expresses the love of God? And down deep, *the* question may be, whether it is put directly or not: Will I be welcome? Or, is your church an inviting church? Is it a safe space? Is it *truly* welcoming?

Wright refers us to the symbols of a culture. Here we might be reminded of a symbol that is important to the Episcopal Church. These days they are going the way of the dinosaur, but for generations the Episcopal Church has had the iconic 'Blue and White sign.' Blue and White signs have been around for decades. We have Blue and White signs on two of the four corners of our property. There were once three others scattered around town, but they really have gone the way of the dinosaur, and, in reality, given the ubiquity of GPS and Google, they are not as necessary as they once were in actually helping people find the church campus. People now can find our church by other means, but we still keep the signs up on the corners of the campus because of what they represent. They remain an iconic symbol of the Episcopal Church conveying an important message. The message on the Blue and White sign—whether you are in Cleveland, Tennessee, or Atlanta, Georgia, or Tempe, Arizona, or Olympia, Washington—is the same: "The Episcopal Church Welcomes You." Words of invitation which have stood the test of time. Words whose meaning has broadened over time. The challenge for local congregations is to make the invitation a reality, to be a truly welcoming, roomy, grace-filled faith community. In the moment that is now so many people *are* searching for a church experience that is both grounded in tradition and responsive to the Zeitgeist wherein so much is shifting, so much is changing.

"The Episcopal Church Welcomes You." To a faith tradition that has deep roots, and yet welcomes the questions that people *are* asking.

"And I, when I am lifted up from the earth, will draw all people to myself." Amen.

---

1. *Webster's Ninth New Collegiate Dictionary* (Springfield, MA: Merriam-Webster Inc., Publishers, 1987), 742.
2. N. T. Wright, *Twelve Months of Sundays: Biblical Meditations on the Christian Years A, B & C* (New York: Morehouse Publishing, 2012), 179.

10
CHRIST IS IN OUR MIDST!

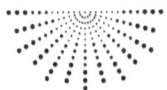

MARK 16:1-8 • 4 APRIL 2021 • EASTER SUNDAY

¹When the sabbath was over, Mary Magdalene, and Mary the mother of James, and Salome bought spices, so that they might go and anoint him. ²And very early on the first day of the week, when the sun had risen, they went to the tomb. ³They had been saying to one another, "Who will roll away the stone for us from the entrance to the tomb?" ⁴When they looked up, they saw that the stone, which was very large, had already been rolled back. ⁵As they entered the tomb, they saw a young man, dressed in a white robe, sitting on the right side; and they were alarmed. ⁶But he said to them, "Do not be alarmed; you are looking for Jesus of Nazareth, who was crucified. He has been raised; he is not here. Look, there is the place they laid him. ⁷But go, tell his disciples and Peter that he is going ahead of you to Galilee; there you will see him, just as he told you." ⁸So they went out and fled from the tomb, for terror and amazement had seized them; and they said nothing to anyone, for they were afraid.

In preparing for this sermon I came across a story out of the Church of England. The story references a small parish church that does not have the services of a full-time priest; the parish relies on supply clergy. The story, from just last year, is that when the visiting priest arrived for the Easter morning service, the church warden saw the priest getting out of his car and ran to meet him in the parking lot. The church warden then said to the visiting priest, on *Easter Sunday*: "Do you believe that God raised our Lord Jesus from the dead?" The visiting priest said: "Yes, I do." To which the church warden responded: "Oh wonderful! The priest we had last year just talked about the coming of spring."

The following is a fact of history. Prior to Jesus of Nazareth, history does not record the name of one other person whom the Roman government crucified. Just let that fact sink in. We know that the Romans practiced crucifixion. This is a well-established fact of history. But prior to Jesus of Nazareth, not one other name is recorded of persons who were crucified. There is nothing trivial regarding this historical reality. The Romans used crucifixion to stamp out a person's life. It was the cruelest, the most inhumane means of execution possible. And it was reserved for the worst of the worst. There is a reason why, prior to Jesus, not a single name is recorded of those who were crucified. The Romans wanted it that way. In our lexicon we talk about having something "expunged" from the record. Under certain circumstances, if certain criteria are met, a criminal conviction can be expunged, can be wiped off the books as if it never happened. What the Roman government sought to do with crucifixion was to expunge a life. The Romans wanted it to be as if that person had never existed.

Regarding the faithful women who went to the tomb on that first Easter morning, Madeleine L'Engle writes: "Everything they believed in had died on the cross with Jesus."[1] For those women, to whom Jesus had meant everything, *everything* they believed in had died on the cross with him. In Jewish theology there was no allowance whatsoever for the idea of the Messiah, God's Anointed One, being betrayed into the hands of a foreign power and executed by that foreign power in the most humiliating, the most inhumane of ways. Nothing in Jewish thinking would have allowed for the possibility of the Messiah having been brutally victimized, and then executed—expunged—by a foreign power. The women were devastated by the reality that their Lord had died.

When I think about those women who went to the tomb in such devastating, such all-consuming grief, to offer spices and to anoint Jesus' body, I cannot help but think of my own mother. I think about her because in 2003 my sister Lee died unexpectedly. All these years later I can still vividly remember watching the love and care with which my mother picked out the dress in which my sister would be buried. I can remember watching my mother being so thoughtful, so careful to pick out the prettiest dress in which my sister's corpse would be laid to rest. What I saw was my mother offering one last and final tangible gesture of love, one last act through which she could express her love for and devotion to her daughter. And that is what the women in our passage were doing that first Easter morning. They took those aromatic spices hoping to anoint Jesus' body in one final, tangible action of love. And in so doing they would simultaneously help to mitigate the smell of the decomposing corpse. They went to the tomb grieving the devastating loss of their Lord who had died.

And the rest, as they say, is history.

Well, yes and no. Yes, the Church makes an historical claim that God having raised Jesus from the dead is an event of history. But the Easter faith does not rest simply on an historical claim. Easter Sunday does not merely commemorate an event of history, a singular moment in time. Today we celebrate Jesus Christ risen and active. Today, and every day, we celebrate Jesus Christ alive and at large in the world.

One of the most prolific biblical scholars of the twentieth century was William Barclay. In commenting on our passage,

Barclay states: "Jesus is not a figure in a book but a living presence. It is not enough to study the story of Jesus like the life of any other great historical figure. We may begin that way but we must end by meeting him."[2] Jesus is not so much someone to discuss as someone to meet. On this Easter Day the Risen Christ meets *us*: Christ risen and active—Christ alive and at large in the world.

One of the great theologians of our time is Rowan Williams, the 104th Archbishop of Canterbury. Williams observes: "Easter marks the event that changes the entire landscape of how we talk about, and think about, and relate to both God and humanity..."[3] Which is a way of saying that Christian faith *is* Easter faith. The lens through which we Christians see the whole of life is that of Easter.

One of the finest preachers of our time is Sam Lloyd, former dean of Washington National Cathedral. From the pulpit of the National Cathedral Sam Lloyd in a sermon for Easter Day proclaimed: "Easter demands that we reframe how we see the world."[4] At all times, and in all circumstances. On *this* Easter Day, in the midst of a global pandemic, and in the midst of social stirring in this country the likes of which we have not seen in fifty years—in this particular moment in history how we reframe the world and our response to the moment that is now is meant to be our Easter faith: the hope, and, ultimately, the joy of Easter.

In the historic moment in which we find ourselves, every day —whether we think consciously about it or not—we each ask ourselves: How do I respond? And: How do *we* respond to this moment in time? As people of faith, where do we turn for guidance? Where do we turn for inspiration?

Of course, when we really think about it, we know the answer to these questions. Our response is meant to be guided by Christ —Christ risen and active—Christ alive and at large in the world. It is the Risen Christ, the Easter Christ, who is our teacher, our inspiration, and our hope. As William Barclay reminds us: Jesus is not someone to discuss so much as someone to meet.

"Alleluia! Christ is risen!" It feels wonderful to say it, does it not? Especially now in these difficult and challenging times. It sounds wonderful. "Alleluia! Christ is risen!" "The Lord is risen indeed! Alleluia!" Beautiful words. Instructive words. Reassuring words. Inspiring words.

"Alleluia! Christ is risen..." is how the most familiar Easter acclamation in Western Christianity begins. But in some quarters of the Eastern Church the celebrant's Easter acclamation is: "Christ is in our midst!" And the people respond: "He is, and always will be!" Amen.

---

1. Madeleine L'Engle, "Waiting for Judas." *Bread and Wine: Readings for Lent and Easter* (Farmington, MA: The Plough Publishing House, 2003), 313.
2. William Barclay, *The Gospel of Mark*. Revised Edition. The Daily Study Bible Series (Louisville: Westminster John Knox Press, 1975), 368.
3. Rowan Williams, *Choose Life: Christmas and Easter Sermons in Canterbury Cathedral* (London: Bloomsbury Publishing, 2013), ix.
4. Samuel T. Lloyd III, *Sermons from the National Cathedral:* Soundings for the Journey (Lanham, MD: Rowman & Littlefield Publishers, 2013), 307.

THE ESSENCE OF THE GOSPEL

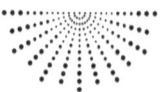

1 JOHN 1:1–2:2 • 11 APRIL 2021
SECOND SUNDAY OF EASTER

¹We declare to you what was from the beginning, what we have heard, what we have seen with our eyes, what we have looked at and touched with our hands, concerning the word of life—²this life was revealed, and we have seen it and testify to it, and declare to you the eternal life that was with the Father and was revealed to us—³we declare to you what we have seen and heard so that you also may have fellowship with us; and truly our fellowship is with the Father and with his Son Jesus Christ. ⁴We are writing these things so that our joy may be complete. ⁵This is the message we have heard from him and proclaim to you, that God is light and in him there is no darkness at all. ⁶If we say that we have fellowship with him while we are walking in darkness, we lie and do not do what is true; ⁷but if we walk in the light as he himself is in the light, we have fellowship with one another, and the blood of Jesus his Son cleanses us from all sin. ⁸If we say that we have no sin, we deceive ourselves, and the truth is not in us. ⁹If we confess our sins, he who is faithful and just will forgive us our sins and cleanse us from all unrighteousness. ¹⁰If we say that we have not sinned, we make him a liar, and his

word is not in us. ¹My little children, I am writing these things to you so that you may not sin. But if anyone does sin, we have an advocate with the Father, Jesus Christ the righteous; ²and he is the atoning sacrifice for our sins, and not for ours only but also for the sins of the whole world.

∽

In his commentary on 1 John 1:8–9, Stephen Smalley writes: "Here is the essence of the Gospel..."[1] It is a strong claim: the *essence* of the Gospel. "If we say that we have no sin, we deceive ourselves, and the truth is not in us. If we confess our sins, he who is faithful and just will forgive us our sins and cleanse us from all unrighteousness." The case can be made that these verses do indeed contain the essence of the Gospel: recognition of our inherent human selfishness, and God's boundless willingness to forgive.

We say the Lord's Prayer as part of every public service of worship in the Episcopal Church. At every Eucharist, of course, but also at every wedding and at every funeral we say the Lord's Prayer. During the worst of the pandemic we replaced Holy Eucharist with Morning Prayer as our main Sunday service. We say the Lord's Prayer in each service of Morning Prayer. In that same period of time we went to Noonday Prayer on Thursdays in place of the Eucharist. In Noonday Prayer we say the Lord's Prayer. *Every* Prayer Book service of worship offered in the Episcopal Church contains the Lord's Prayer.

Every time we pray the Lord's Prayer we say these words: "And forgive us our trespasses, as we forgive those who trespass against us." Of course, one of the jewels of the Anglican tradition is *The Book of Common Prayer*, and the title of the book is foundationally important to our understanding of it: The Book of *Common* Prayer. "Common" in the sense of communal, shared prayer. In his commentary on 1 John 1:8–9, Daniel L. Akin writes: "the true condition for fellowship is the confession of our sins."[2] Another strong and thought-provoking claim. If we are going to have genuine fellowship with each other, true community, we have to be willing to acknowledge that we all make mistakes; we all drift off of the path that leads us closest to God. And thus for our experience of community to be all it can be we all have to acknowledge our propensity to make mistakes. A necessary condition of genuine fellowship is for me to recognize that I am not meant to stand in judgment of you, and for you to recognize that you are not meant to stand in judgment of me. Together, *in community*, we confess our mistakes, and together, *in community*, we receive forgiveness.

Our *common* prayer comes from our *common*, our shared humanity. We all stand before God as imperfect human beings who, even in our sinfulness, are offered God's compassionate mercy and grace. Particularly now amidst this pandemic, and amidst social stirring the likes of which this country has not seen in fifty years, we come to church in need of hearing good news, *the* Good News which offers us hope even in the midst of so many vexing challenges.

Again, 1 John 1:8–9, the essence of the Gospel: "If we say that we have no sin, we deceive ourselves, and the truth is not in us. If we confess our sins, he who is faithful and just will forgive us our sins and cleanse us from all unrighteousness." One of the great thinkers of the ancient world was Philo of Alexandria (c. 20 BCE —c. 50 CE). Philo once observed: "Perfection and an absence of deficiency are found in God alone. But deficiency and imperfection exist in *every* (emphasis added) man."[3] Here Philo, like the author of 1 John, reminds us of the importance of humility. We all come from the same earth, and we all share in the frailties of our common humanity.

The Johannine Epistles are tucked away in the back of the New Testament. Similarly located is the Epistle of James. In 5:16a James writes: "Therefore confess your sins to one another, and pray for one another, so that you may be healed."

We live in a deeply divisive time. We all sense and feel the tension(s) in our culture. Many preexisting and long-simmering divisions have been brought to a boil during the pandemic. In recent months I have chosen to do a deep dive into some of our 18th-century American history. When we engage in serious study of our history we are forced to recognize that American life has suffered from deep divisions from the start. Our experiment in democracy has been imperfect from the beginning.

There have always been tensions in American culture along racial and other socioeconomic lines. One of the differences between previous eras and now is that people used to get their news in smaller, more manageable bites from a handful of agreed-upon sources. First from newspapers, then from radio as well. In the early days of television, most of America watched the evening news 'together' on the handful of network channels available. But now, with the proliferation of cable news and social media, we can get news twenty-four hours a day, seven days a week in a constant flow, and thus we are being reminded endlessly of the tensions, the stresses, and the anxieties of the moment that is now. Similar tensions have, in reality, been present all throughout American history but are now in our face 24/7. There is a deepening cultural anger present across the political spectrum. Simultaneously there is a tendency toward righteous indignation across the same political spectrum. In the cauldron of so much stress, anger, and fear, the question ever before us as followers of Christ is: How do we best respond?

So back to 1 John. The epistle was written in a moment when the early Christian congregation to which the letter was addressed was experiencing a split over doctrine. Imagine that, Christians arguing with one another over doctrine! 1 John was written to address a split in an early Christian congregation, and it is in the context of tension, frustration, and anger that John writes: "If *we* (emphasis added) say that we have no sin, we deceive ourselves, and the truth is not in us." Which is a pastoral way of saying: None of us can be right all the time. None of us can have *all* of the truth on our side *all* of the time. If we say that we have no sin

—if we think that we unfailingly occupy the high ground, and that we are always in the right—we deceive ourselves. If we say that we have no sin, says John, we are kidding ourselves! But if we confess our sins. If we will have some humility. If we can be vulnerable enough to acknowledge and admit our human frailties to God...

The historical context of 1 John is crucial to its interpretation. The beautiful and deeply spiritual words of our passage were written to address tensions and, no doubt, bitter disappointment within a Christian community which was meant to be at unity with itself. To the frustration and anger of the moment John's counsel was: Have some humility. No side gets it exactly right all the time. And remember to see other members of the community not as enemies, but as sisters and brothers in Christ.

From Navajo culture comes the timeless wisdom: "Always remember, when you are pointing your finger at someone else, at least three fingers are pointing back at you." If we say that we have no sin, we deceive ourselves. Amen.

---

1. Stephen Smalley, *Word Biblical Commentary: 1, 2, 3 John*. Volume 51 (Revised Edition). Bruce M. Metzger, David A. Hubbard and Glenn W. Barker, General Editors (Nashville: Thomas Nelson, 2007), 38.
2. Daniel L. Akin, *The American Commentary: 1, 2, 3 John*. Volume 38. E. Ray Clendenen, General Editor (Nashville: Broadman and Holman Publishers, 2001), 74.
3. Robert W. Yarbrough, *1–3 John*. Baker Exegetical Commentary on the New Testament. Robert W. Yarbrough and Robert H. Stein, Editors (Grand Rapids: Baker Academic, 2008), 60.

12

I SEE YOU

1 JOHN 3:1–7 • 18 APRIL 2021
THIRD SUNDAY OF EASTER

¹See what love the Father has given us, that we should be called children of God; and that is what we are. The reason the world does not know us is that it did not know him. ²Beloved, we are God's children now; what we will be has not yet been revealed. What we do know is this: when he is revealed, we will be like him, for we will see him as he is. ³And all who have this hope in him purify themselves, just as he is pure. ⁴Everyone who commits sin is guilty of lawlessness; sin is lawlessness. ⁵You know that he was revealed to take away sins, and in him there is no sin. ⁶No one who abides in him sins; no one who sins has either seen him or known him. ⁷Little children, let no one deceive you. Everyone who does what is right is righteous, just as he is righteous.

～

We are now past the one-year mark of what will prove to be an unforgettable chapter in our history. It all began with the onset of a global pandemic, the likes of which we have not seen in 100 years. Then came the social stirring following the deaths of Ahmaud Arbery and George Floyd; and even today, we remain in a season of social unrest.

Beginning in mid-March 2020, our worship services began to be offered in a significantly different format: online only. As soon as it seemed safe we, along with many other churches, began a gradual return to in-person worship. During all of this, as rector of the parish I would say periodically to both our staff and to parishioners: "There is no playbook for this." Or, "There is no script…" For over a year now, how the church operates has had to be reimagined, including the most important thing we do: corporate worship.

Throughout all of this people have been good to offer encouragement to those of us on the church staff. I want you all to know that we are deeply grateful for the many gestures of support offered during this challenging season. We are grateful for *every* gesture of support and encouragement, but in preparing this address two e-mails in particular that I received in the last year stuck out in my mind. On two different occasions during the thick of the pandemic, from two different parishioners I received e-mail messages that said in part: "I see you." Each person went on to say, in effect, I see what you are doing. I see what the church is doing. I see the lengths to which the church is going to minister to its people. *I see you.* I will admit that, in real time, I lingered over those two e-mails, taking to heart the deep thought and care which lay behind the words, "I see you."

In 1 John 3:1 we read: "See what love the Father has given us, that we should be called children of God; and that is what we are." The verse begins with: *See.* In the Greek it is imperative. The Greek can also be translated: *Look.* Either way, it is an imperative. David Jackman writes about this verse: "'Look,' 'See!' The force is that we need to take time to contemplate this love and allow its reality to sink down into the depths of our being. It is meant to take our breath away; to startle and amaze us so that we are left gasping. 'What sort of love is this?'"[1] In 3:1 the author is using language that will get his readers' attention in order for them to focus on the depth of God's love. *See... Look...*

The "what love..." involves the Greek word *potapos*, which can also be translated as "great" or "lavish." 1 John 3:1 can be rendered: "See what lavish love the Father has given us..." A word study of *potapos* reveals that it makes reference to foreignness. What the Greek is seeking to convey is: God's love is of such depth, such quality, that it is as if it has come to us from a foreign land. *Potapos* occurs two other times in the Gospels. In Mark 13:1 we read: "As [Jesus] came out of the temple, one of his disciples said to him, 'Look, Teacher, what large stones and what large buildings!'" The disciples were 'country boys' from Galilee, and in the big city were in awe of the sheer size and scale of the Temple. *Look, Teacher, what large stones and what large buildings!* We might put it: This isn't Kansas anymore.

The second example is from Matthew 8:27, the Stilling of the Storm. Matthew 8:27 reads: "They were amazed, saying, 'What sort of man is this, that even the winds and the sea obey him?'" *What sort of man is this*? Here again the disciples are saying in effect: We've never seen anything like this. Who is this man?

Back to 1 John 3:1, where *potapos* is employed in an attempt to convey a sense of the depth, the reach, of God's love. In translating 3:1 Stephen Smalley renders it: "Consider how lavish is the love that the Father has showered upon us..."[2] Smalley then comments: "God's love is unbelievably exuberant."[3] In a similar vein, in referring to Divine love's largess, Mark Oakley has written of God's "reckless mercy."[4] *Potapos*.

In interpreting 3:1 it is crucial that we hear the imperative in: "See what love the Father has given us, that we should be called children of God, and that is what we are." You and I, and all others like us: normal people, capable of both great goodness and grievous mistakes; we are the beloved, lavishly graced children of God.

Back to where we started. What John is doing in this brief but deeply instructive passage is to say that God's message to us is: *I see you.* I see you, and I love you. *See what love the Father has given us, that we should be called children of God...* In her commentary on 3:1 Marianne Meye Thompson writes: "'Calling' means more than naming. It means the inauguration of a relationship, of a reality that can best be pictured by the metaphor of being God's own children."[5] In other words, we are not merely told (passive) that we are beloved. We are called into relationship (imperative) with the giver of such extravagantly generous love. Divine love here is not merely a theological concept, a lavish but abstract notion that has no meaningful connection to reality. The great love to which we are called in 1 John invites us into a personal, intimate, and collective relationship. *I see you* is the message of 1 John 3:1. I see you, and I love you in ways beyond your imagining.

Daniel L. Akin writes of 3:1: "The imperative [See! Look!] calls for direct attention and reflection upon the amazing love God has bestowed upon his children."[6] There are different levels of love, all of which have their place. But the love of God proclaimed in Christian theology is a love the depth of which we have trouble even imagining, let alone comprehending. Akin goes on: "God's is a love that works visible, transforming results in the lives of its recipients."[7] And: "those who believe take on more than a title..."[8] Good News indeed, especially in this historic time of pandemic *and* social reckoning. Good News—Gospel—that carries with it an imperative. Amen.

---

1. David Jackman, *The Message of John's Letters*. The Bible Speaks Today. J. A. Motyer and John R. W. Stott, Series Editors (Downers Grove, IL: InterVarsity Press, 1988), 81.
2. Stephen Smalley, *Word Biblical Commentary: 1, 2, 3 John*. Volume 51 (Revised Edition). Bruce M. Metzger, David A. Hubbard and Glenn W. Barker, General Editors (Nashville: Thomas Nelson, Inc., 2007), 131.
3. *Ibid.*, 133.
4. Joel W. Huffstetler, *Practical Faith and Active Love: Meditations on the Epistle of James* (Berkeley: Apocryphile Press, 2020), i.
5. Marianne Meye Thompson, *1–3 John*. The IVP New Testament Commentary Series. Grant R. Osborne, Series Editor (Downers Grove, IL: InterVarsity Press, 1992), 88.

6. Daniel L. Akin, *The New American Commentary: 1, 2, 3 John*. Volume 38. E. Ray Clendenen, General Editor (Nashville: Broadman and Holman Publishers, 2001), 132.
7. *Ibid.*, 133.
8. *Ibid.*

13
AS CLEAR AS IT GETS

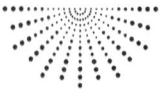

1 JOHN 4:7–21 • 2 MAY 2021
FIFTH SUNDAY OF EASTER

⁷Beloved, let us love one another, because love is from God; everyone who loves is born of God and knows God. ⁸Whoever does not love does not know God, for God is love. ⁹God's love was revealed among us in this way: God sent his only Son into the world so that we might live through him. ¹⁰In this is love, not that we loved God but that he loved us and sent his Son to be the atoning sacrifice for our sins. ¹¹Beloved, since God loved us so much, we also ought to love one another. ¹²No one has ever seen God; if we love one another, God lives in us, and his love is perfected in us. ¹³By this we know that we abide in him and he in us, because he has given us of his Spirit. ¹⁴And we have seen and do testify that the Father has sent his Son as the Savior of the world. ¹⁵God abides in those who confess that Jesus is the Son of God, and they abide in God. ¹⁶So we have known and believe the love that God has for us. God is love, and those who abide in love abide in God, and God abides in them. ¹⁷Love has been perfected among us in this: that we may have boldness on the day of judgment, because as he is, so are we in this world. ¹⁸There is no fear in love, but perfect love casts out fear; for fear

has to do with punishment, and whoever fears has not reached perfection in love. ¹⁹We love because he first loved us. ²⁰Those who say, "I love God," and hate their brothers or sisters, are liars; for those who do not love a brother or sister whom they have seen, cannot love God whom they have not seen. ²¹The commandment we have from him is this: those who love God must love their brothers and sisters also.

~

One of my go-to sayings is: If it looks like a duck, and walks like a duck, and quacks like a duck, it might be a duck. While I am careful not to wear it out, there is a lot of truth in that saying. Many years ago I was standing in a long line waiting to get into an iconic restaurant. As a group of patrons made their way out of the restaurant, one of them said to those of us standing in line to gain entrance: "The food is worth standing in line for." One of the people waiting in line had mentioned that he was the president of a leading university in the northeast United States and was on vacation. Given this man's bearing and his vocabulary, his being a university president seemed believable. So again, the person coming out of the restaurant had said: "The food is worth standing in line for"—to which the university president responded: "I don't know what that means." The man who had said it then repeated slower and more deliberately: "It means *the food is worth standing in line for.*" You may know the phrase, the paralysis of analysis. Sometimes we overthink things. Sometimes we are too much in our head when what should be obvious is right before us, if we will but see it.

In commenting on 1 John 4:7–21 Cally Hammond writes: "Not everything about the Bible is difficult. When scripture speaks straightforwardly, we sometimes shrink from the plain sense..."[1] A good insight. Some things in the Bible *are* clear, and when the teaching is clear we should not overcomplicate it. If it looks like a duck, and walks like a duck, and quacks like a duck, it just might be a duck. Thankfully, not everything in Scripture is hard to understand, and thus Hammond says of 1 John 4:12 in particular that it is "as clear as it gets: 'If we love one aother, God lives in us, and his love is perfected in us.'"[2] Her point could not be clearer: 1 John 4:12 simply means what it says.

She goes on to note: "The measure of all Christian actions must be 1 John 4:21: 'Those who love God must love their brothers [and sisters] also.'"[3] Another strong insight. The measure of *all* Christian actions must be 1 John 4:21. In context, our passage is referring to church members; church members are called unequivocally to love one another. To be sure, what we are taught in church is meant to be carried into the world, but it begins *in church*, the understanding that if we claim to love God, then we are to love our brothers and sisters in Christ also.

Love is clearly the theme of 1 John. In his commentary on our passage N. T. Wright states: "In the New Testament, 'love' regularly describes not so much how people feel as what they do."[4] In its New Testament context the word *love (agape)* does not primarily connote a feeling or a concept. Love in the New Testament is not so much about an emotion. Instead, it connotes action. The two are inextricably linked—our love of God leads to action in God's name. Wright also observes: "Love incarnate must be the badge that the Christian community wears, the sign not only of who they are but of who their God is."[5] Love incarnate—love in action—is who the Church is meant to be.

If you know where this is headed, feel free to join in: *The main thing is to keep the main thing the main thing.* Again, 1 John 4:12b: "if we love one another, God lives in us, and his love is perfected in us." And 1 John 4:21: "those who love God must love their brothers and sisters also."

In 1 John 4:18 we find: "There is no fear in love, but perfect love casts out fear; for fear has to do with punishment, and whoever fears has not reached perfection in love." Perfection here carries with it a sense of spiritual maturity, not faultless morality.

A mature Christian's primary orientation should be toward love, not fear.

A brief story. From early 1995 until early 2003, I served on the pastoral staff of St. Paul's Episcopal Church in downtown Chattanooga. In many ways those eight-and-a-half years were wonderful. I met Debbie on my second Sunday there, and we got married in November, 1997, in what parishioners called "The Royal Wedding." She and I did not call it that(!), but we heard it. I first encountered the writings of Michael Mayne during the St. Paul's years and have spent a significant portion of my career bringing his previously unpublished material to light. At St. Paul's, Debbie and I made many friends who are friends to this day: dear friends whom we love deeply. But not everything was wonderful for me in those years. During that time my life-long tendency to anxiety, my doggedly nagging habit of being constantly and harshly self-critical, snowballed amidst the stresses of ministry in that large and fast-paced parish, and what had for years been a nuisance, a manageable thorn in the flesh, mushroomed into a full-blown personal and vocational crisis.

I made every effort not to let anyone in the parish know that I was struggling, and to my knowledge, no one ever did. It was all internalized, and I worked tirelessly to maintain the appearance that everything was fine, which was both all-consuming and exhausting. It is exhausting keeping up appearances when, in reality, nothing is at it appears on the surface. Things were so difficult for me that, without anyone else knowing it, I was actually considering leaving parish ministry. There was a time in my career when I actively thought about backing away from the public eye, getting a pastoral counseling license, and doing pastoral counseling full-time in a private setting. This was a serious thought for months. But at just the right time, a doctor of mine, my allergist(!), recommended a therapist, and in due course I entered into a fifteen-week treatment module combining cognitive therapy and hypnosis—a re-programming of my thought world. As the first session began, I sat down, looked the therapist in the eyes and said: "Given what I do for a living, I'm a little embarrassed to be here. But I need help." Fortunately, he was a gentle, kind and knowledgeable man, and old enough to have been my grandfather. He said to me: "Everybody needs a little help once in a while. You have nothing to be embarrassed about." I remember his kindness to this day.

His first therapeutic question was: "Are you a perfectionist?" That was *the* first question, and I can remember my answer to this day: "I don't really think so." He smiled, and then responded: "Well, let's talk about that." And thus, at a genuine crossroads in my life, began fifteen transformative weeks of introspection and therapy during which I finally began to come to terms with the realities of my anxiety-prone personality.

During this intensive fifteen-week period, Debbie and I would leave town at every possible opportunity for me to get away from the phone, away from the constant voicemails, and away from my seemingly endless "to do" list. On one of those brief trips we were in Pigeon Forge, and there came a point when I went into a small Christian bookshop that was tucked away in the far corner of an outlet mall. Just a small Christian bookstore which would have been easy to miss amidst all the larger, much glitzier stores. Near the cashier's station was a stand of cards—devotional cards—and of all the cards on offer, one the bright yellow-green color of a tennis ball caught my eye. All that the card had on it was a smiley face and a caption: "There is no fear in love, but perfect love casts out fear." A portion of 1 John 4:18. And somehow in *that* moment *those words* made sense to me like few words ever had. In that life-altering moment those words broke through, and, in time, with the accumulating benefits of therapy and the clarity of that one verse of Scripture, for the first time I started feeling hopeful again. Somehow, in that moment, 1 John 4:18 started unlocking in me a capacity for self-forgiveness and self-love that I had never allowed myself to feel. In that one moment, in a small Christian bookshop I had wandered into, after many months of deeply internalized struggle there dawned a ray of hope, and what then began to happen incrementally—step by step, day by day—was nothing short of a spiritual and vocational resurrection.

I am speaking to you from the depth of my soul. 1 John 4:18 has helped to redirect my life, and has helped me finally to receive for myself the love of God that for years I had been better at proclaiming than feeling. *There is no fear in love; but perfect love casts out fear.*

Outside of the Bible, and *The Book of Common Prayer*, one of my favorite devotional books is *A Common Prayer* by Michael Leunig. I want to finish with two brief passages from the book. First: "There are only two feelings, love and fear. There are only two languages, love and fear. There are only two activities, love and fear. There are only two motives, two procedures, two frameworks, two results. Love and fear. Love and Fear."[6] And then this clear and effective reminder that the main thing is to keep the main thing the main thing. "Love one another and you will be happy. It is as simple and as difficult as that. There is no other way."[7] Amen.

---

1. Cally Hammond, "5th Sunday of Easter." *Church Times*. 22 April 2021.
   https://www.churchtimes.co.uk/articles/2021/30-april/faith/sunday-s-readings/5th-sunday-of-easter
2. *Ibid.*
3. *Ibid.*
4. N. T. Wright, *Twelve Months of Sundays: Biblical Meditations on the Christian Years A, B & C* (New York: Morehouse Publishing, 2012), 193.
5. N. T. Wright, *The Early Christian Letters for Everyone: James, Peter, John, and Judah* (Louisville: Westminster John Knox Press, 2011), 158.
6. Michael Leunig, *A Common Prayer* (North Blackburn, Victoria, Australia: CollinsDove Publishers, 1990), unnumbered page.
7. *Ibid.*

14

THE SPIRIT BLOWS WHERE IT CHOOSES

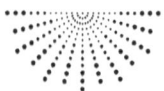

ACTS 10:44–48 • 9 MAY 2021
SIXTH SUNDAY OF EASTER

⁴⁴While Peter was still speaking, the Holy Spirit fell upon all who heard the word. ⁴⁵The circumcised believers who had come with Peter were astounded that the gift of the Holy Spirit had been poured out even on the Gentiles, ⁴⁶for they heard them speaking in tongues and extolling God. Then Peter said, ⁴⁷"Can anyone withhold the water for baptizing these people who have received the Holy Spirit just as we have?" ⁴⁸So he ordered them to be baptized in the name of Jesus Christ. Then they invited him to stay for several days.

∼

In his commentary on Acts 10:44–48, Carl Holladay writes that the contents of the passage represent: "the breakthrough event...of the early Christian mission."[1] A strong statement. Acts 10:44–48 represents the *breakthrough* (emphasis added) event of the earliest Christian mission. And in his commentary on the passage James D. G. Dunn notes: "the decisive *breakthrough* (emphasis added) of God's blessing to the nations has taken place."[2] Acts 10:44–48 depicts what has been referred to as the

"Gentile Pentecost." In *The HarperCollins Study Bible* the section heading over our passage reads: "Gentiles Receive the Holy Spirit."

Our passage fits within a larger literary context. To get the full meaning of Acts 10:44–48 it is good to read 10:1–11:18 as a unit. In brief, what is happening is this: a Roman army officer named Cornelius has a vision of a prophet coming to visit his household. Simultaneously, a prophet, Peter, falls into a trance and has a vision of a picnic where food of all kinds is understood to be equally appropriate for the occasion. This may not sound like much until we place it in historical and theological context. What Peter's vision represents is a first-century Jew coming to understand and acknowledge that *all* food is worthy to be consumed. What is happening here theologically is that Peter's vision paves the way for Gentiles to be included in table fellowship with Jews, as the traditional Jewish dietary laws have come to be superseded by the universal significance of the risen Christ. So, a Roman soldier has a vision of a prophet coming to his household, and that prophet has a vision of *all* people being able to sit down together and have table fellowship with one another. The end result of the two visions comes to fruition in 10:44–48.

Peter does, in fact, meet Cornelius and his household in Caesarea, and he shares with them the Gospel. Acts 10:44: "While Peter was still speaking, the Holy Spirit fell upon all who heard the word." And thus the description of our passage as the Gentile Pentecost. Then the passage continues: "The circumcised believers who had come with Peter were astounded that the gift of the Holy Spirit had been poured out even on the Gentiles, for they heard them speaking in tongues and extolling God." The precise wording is key here. The *same* Holy Spirit that the Jesus Movement experienced at Pentecost is now clearly evident in this Gentile household, witnessing to the universal significance of the risen Christ.

And then the passage continues: "Then Peter said, 'Can anyone withhold the water for baptizing these people who have received the

Holy Spirit just as we have?'" Here we remember Peter's vision of a picnic where all food is equally appropriate in God's eyes, which signifies that Gentiles and Jews can sit together, can dine together, can *be* together. Peter sees the Holy Spirit manifest in this Gentile household, and he then asks the obvious question: Is there any reason why these people should not be baptized if they are experiencing the same gift from God that we have experienced? And of course the answer is: No. For Peter, there is no longer any valid theological reason why Gentiles cannot be baptized. And then we come to verse 48a: "So [Peter] ordered them to be baptized in the name of Jesus Christ." This *is* the breakthrough event in the earliest Christian mission.

In the Hebrew Scriptures we read in Joel 2:28: "Then afterward I will pour my spirit on all flesh..." Here is prophecy that the relationship the Jewish nation has with God will come to be shared by all of humanity. Through God's covenantal relationship with Israel, *all* of humanity will come to understand that the Covenant is in fact open to all.

The Jewish Christian experience begins with Easter: the empty tomb and the appearances of the risen Christ. The movement gains momentum at Pentecost through the outpouring of the Holy Spirit. And then in due course the Spirit's work spreads into the Gentile world. Cornelius and his household represent the Gentile world: a *Roman* soldier and his Gentile household, living in Caesarea, the Roman capital city of Judea. The Holy Spirit is breaking out from Jesus' early followers and will now spread from Caesarea to the ends of the earth. Acts 10:44–48 can be read in a matter of seconds, but it captures for us crucially important biblical and salvation history: the beginning of the 'walls' coming down and the 'gates' being flung open. Here we see the beginning of inclusion, the work of the Spirit that continues to this day.

And then the final bit of the passage, 10:48b: "Then they [the Roman household] invited him [Peter] to stay for several days." Let us please see what is happening here in its deepest significance. What we have before us in this 'breakthrough' event is the blending of cultures. A Jewish fisherman, one of Jesus' closest friends, is now able to sit down at table with a Roman soldier and his household. Before Easter, this would have been highly countercultural. Just try to imagine such a scene playing out in the days between Jesus' triumphal entry into Jerusalem and his crucifixion only days later. But in light of the Pentecost—the outpouring of the Holy Spirit—what was once impossible is now happening. Formerly bitter enemies can become cherished friends through the Spirit of God.

One of the great preachers of recent years is Will Willimon, who writes in his commentary on our passage: "Conversion is the beginning of the Christian journey, not its final destination."[3] The confession, "Jesus is Lord," is not the end of the journey; it is only the beginning of our relationship with God in Christ. And thus we have every reason to believe that Cornelius and his household invited Peter to stay with them so that Peter could teach them more about Jesus. Let us at least try to imagine the extraordinary situation Cornelius and his household were in: being able to speak with one of Jesus' closest friends in the privacy of their own home.

In historical context, Peter and Cornelius would have been natural enemies only a short time before the events portrayed in our passage. But now, in the light of Pentecost, a Roman army officer and his household and one of Jesus' closest followers can sit down together in full fellowship because the same Holy Spirit has been experienced by both.

All of this reminds us of a pivotal verse in the Gospel of John. Jesus is speaking with Nicodemus when we read in 3:8: "The wind (which can also be translated as "Spirit") blows where it chooses, and you hear the sound of it, but you do not know where it comes from or where it goes." Again, what we see in Acts 10:44–48 is the beginning of inclusion, the breaking down of barriers. It is only the beginning and, to be sure, the work goes on even today. But with time, through selfless, Christ-inspired love, with openness of mind and heart, and with *conversation*, enemies can become friends.

The following is a brief story about possibilities. In 2009, Debbie and I had the privilege of traveling to Greece for a month, as I was privileged to be visiting preacher at St. Paul's Anglican Church in the heart of Athens. While there I served with a wonderful Anglican priest named Malcolm Bradshaw, for whom I retain the deepest respect. On the evening of Ascension Day, after no one else(!) showed up for the 6:00 p.m. Ascension Eucharist, a woman walked in off the street and asked us some basic questions about the church. She was polite and engaging, as were we. We were glad to give her basic information about the Church of England and what the local parish in Athens offered. She was very respectful in hearing all of that, and then she said: "Thank you very much indeed, but what I'm really looking for, I think, is an internet church." Keep in mind, this was 2009. *Thank you very much indeed, but I think I'm really looking for an internet church.* And then she walked off. As the woman gradually moved out of earshot Fr. Malcolm scoffed: "An internet church. How ridiculous!" Full disclosure—I agreed with him.

Fast-forward to the pandemic and the (not-so) temporary suspension of in-person worship. In that challenging time we in the Church as a whole began to realize that the internet could help to keep us connected. Eventually we began to realize that not only could it help to keep *us* connected, it could also expand our reach. All these months later we continue to learn what possibilities there are now that we are connected to nearly anyone in the world who has a computer. In 2009, neither Malcolm nor I could see it. But now, in 2021... The Spirit continues its work, and, over time, more and more barriers are crumbling. More and more, though, sadly, not all.

Recently I offered a course in-person and online on a book by Michael Mayne titled, *A Year Lost and Found*. At the conclusion of the course I said to our staff: "Let's do some analysis. I want to know who, outside of Cleveland, has been 'attending' the class online, and their physical location." So we did some digging; we did a deep dive into the metrics. Here is a brief summary of what we found. Outside of Cleveland and Bradley County, we know that people viewed the class in Canton, North Carolina; Franklin, Tennessee; Knoxville, Tennessee; Nashville, Tennessee; Atlanta, Georgia; Ellicott City, Maryland; Pittsburgh, Pennsylvania; Westbrook, Connecticut; and Toronto, Ontario. We even got a smiley face from Perth in Western Australia. A class offered from this local church via the internet reached as far as Australia.

It is a new day. There are so many new and fresh—*breakthrough*—possibilities before us. The Spirit blows where it chooses. Amen.

---

1. Carl R. Holladay. "Sixth Sunday of Easter." *Preaching Through the Christian Year (Year B): A Comprehensive Commentary on the Lectionary*. Fred B. Craddock, John H. Hayes, Carl R. Holladay, Gene M. Tucker, Contributors (Harrisburg, PA: Trinity Press International, 1993), 261.
2. James D. G. Dunn. *The Acts of the Apostles* (Grand Rapids: William B. Eerdmans Publishing Company, 1996), 145.
3. William H. Willimon. *Acts*. Interpretation: A Bible Commentary for Teaching and Preaching. James L. Mays, Editor (Atlanta: John Knox Press, 1988), 103.

15

FIGHTING FOR HUMAN RIGHTS ON EARTH

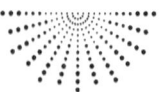

1 JOHN 5:9–13 • 16 MAY 2021
SEVENTH SUNDAY OF EASTER

⁹If we receive human testimony, the testimony of God is greater; for this is the testimony of God that he has testified to his Son. ¹⁰Those who believe in the Son of God have the testimony in their hearts. Those who do not believe in God have made him a liar by not believing in the testimony that God has given concerning his Son. ¹¹And this is the testimony: God gave us eternal life, and this life is in his Son. Whoever has the Son has life; ¹²whoever does not have the Son of God does not have life. ¹³I write these things to you who believe in the name of the Son of God, so that you may know that you have eternal life.

∽

The term "eternal life" occurs in the second verse of 1 John, and in the penultimate verse of the epistle (5:20). And in 5:11: "And this is the testimony: God gave us eternal life, and this life is in his Son." For most of us, when we hear the term "eternal life" we may instinctively think of the afterlife. But in the Greek of the New Testament "eternal Life" does not simply mean life in the hereafter.

It is essential that we read Holy Scripture with a sense of the historical context out of which it arises. Christianity emerged out of a Jewish context. Jesus and his first followers were Jews, and on a daily basis they would have spoken Aramaic, a Semitic language. But, due in large part to the missionary efforts of Paul, Christianity spread primarily in Gentile territory, and thus the books of the New Testament were first written in Greek. In order to understand the term "eternal life" in its New Testament context, we must have a sense of the Greek of that time and place. What did "eternal life" mean to Greek-speaking people in the first century?

Judith Lieu writes regarding our passage that "eternal life" is: "a present possession because it is the inevitable corollary of a present relationship."[1] "Eternal life" in the Greek of the New Testament does not refer only, or even primarily, to life after death. In the New Testament, "eternal life" means an enhanced experience, an enhanced quality of life in the here and now based on a follower's relationship *in the present* with Jesus.

Carl Holladay writes regarding "eternal life" in 1 John: "experiencing it is not postponed until after we die; by believing fully in the Son we are thrust into this 'eternal life' here and now."[2] Believing in Jesus Christ meant not just the promise of the afterlife with God. It meant that life in the present was transformed.

In commenting on our passage Stephen Smalley observes: "'Eternal' life is qualitative, not quantitative; it is the highest *kind* of spiritual and moral life, irrespective of time, that God enables the believer to share in relationship with Jesus."[3] The point here is that scholars are clear—in the Greek of the New Testament "eternal life" is not just a promise for after we die; "eternal life" starts *now* in relationship with Jesus Christ. Eternal life manifests in the here and now in *quality* of life. So, back to Lieu's point. Eternal life is a *present possession* because it is the inevitable corollary of a *present relationship*. In other words, eternal life is not just a spiritual life insurance policy! Eternal life for the author of 1 John includes the here and now.

While driving, I sometimes listen to "soothing radio"—The

Spa Channel—on Sirius XM. That said, I hasten to add that there are still times when I listen to classic rock! But more often than not these days I listen to news, and while pulling out of the church parking lot this past Thursday afternoon I began to hear the reports of the change in CDC guidelines regarding the mask mandate for those fully vaccinated. To be sure, the mask mandate and the wider realities of the pandemic require a layered, nuanced conversation. And that layered, nuanced conversation is not the stuff of a Sunday sermon. That said, Thursday, May 13, 2021, is an historic day in the life of this country, whatever may happen going forward.

I just happened to be the speaker this past Friday morning at Men's Prayer Breakfast, and as the group gathered one could just feel that a cloud had lifted. And in meeting as a staff later that morning to talk about the new guidelines, the three of us who are full-time—Andrea, Isaac and I—met in my office without masks for the first time in over a year. For the first time in over a year we sat where we normally sit and saw each other's full faces. So whatever the future may bring, and however layered and nuanced responsible conversations about COVID have to be going forward, we *are* in the midst of a time of renewed hope in this country. We know that the pandemic is global, and that conditions vary widely from place to place even within our own country. But in *this* place, this time is one of renewed hope.

Later in the day on Thursday I made routine stops at CVS and the Post Office while running normal, everyday errands, and given the announcement earlier in the day—and thus seeing a lot fewer masks—in those otherwise normal comings and goings I could feel that we in this region really are moving forward into a time of renewed hope. Which brings us back to 1 John 5 and "eternal life." Again, John uses it as early as 1:2, and as late as the penultimate verse of the entire epistle. *Eternal life* for John refers to quality of life in the here and now grounded in our relationship with Jesus Christ. Eternal life in Christ is not merely a promise for the future. It is also meant to inform how we live in the moment that is now.

The Johannine Epistles bear a clear relationship to the Gospel of John, though we cannot be sure regarding the authorship of all four documents. Whether the same John wrote all four documents, or whether 'John the elder' wrote the Gospel and 1 John and a student of his wrote 2 John and 3 John, we cannot know for sure. But the Epistles of John bear a clear and close relationship to the Gospel of John. And thus it is important for us to be reminded that in the Gospel of John, in 10:10b, the author records Jesus as having said: "I came that they may have life, and have it abundantly."

We have talked about the importance of historical context in seeking to interpret faithfully a text that is 2,000 years old. But at the same time Holy Scripture is a living and breathing word, and whatever its historical context, we are always meant to apply Scripture's teaching to the here and now. *So what*? What does the ancient word mean to us in the moment that is now? On this note, Cally Hammond observes in a summary comment on our passage: "Christian faith is sometimes criticized for offering, instead of good things in this life, 'pie in the sky when you die.' That phrase comes from a song attacking preachers who promised blessings in heaven instead of fighting for human rights on earth."[4] Amen.

---

1. Judith M. Lieu. *I, II, & III John*. The New Testament Library. C. Clifton Black, M. Eugene Boring and John T. Carroll, Editorial Board (Louisville: Westminster John Knox Press, 2008), 219.
2. Carl R. Holladay. "1 John 5:9-13." *Preaching Through the Christian Year (Year B): A Comprehensive Commentary on the Lectionary*. Fred B. Craddock, John H. Hayes, Carl R. Holladay, Gene M. Tucker, Contributors (Harrisburg, PA: Trinity Press International, 1993), 276.
3. Stephen Smalley. *Word Biblical Commentary: 1, 2, 3 John*. Volume 51 (Revised Edition). Bruce M. Metzger, David A. Hubbard and Glenn W. Barker, General Editors (Nashville: Thomas Nelson, 2007), 274.
4. Cally Hammond, "7th Sunday of Easter." *Church Times*. 06 May 2021. The

song quoted is "The Preacher and the Slave," by Joe Hill sung by Pete Seeger, Utah Phillips, and many others.

16
A TIME OF SOUL SEARCHING FOR US ALL

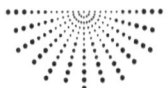

ACTS 2:1–21 • 23 MAY 2021
PENTECOST SUNDAY

¹When the day of Pentecost had come, they were all together in one place. ²And suddenly from heaven there came a sound like the rush of a violent wind, and it filled the entire house where they were sitting. ³Divided tongues, as of fire, appeared among them, and a tongue rested on each of them. ⁴All of them were filled with the Holy Spirit and began to speak in other languages, as the Spirit gave them ability. ⁵Now there were devout Jews from every nation under heaven living in Jerusalem. ⁶And at this sound the crowd gathered and was bewildered, because each one heard them speaking in the native language of each. ⁷Amazed and astonished, they asked, "Are not all these who are speaking Galileans? ⁸And how is it that we hear, each of us, in our own native language? ⁹Parthians, Medes, Elamites, and residents of Mesopotamia, Judea and Cappadocia, Pontus and Asia, ¹⁰Phrygia and Pamphylia, Egypt and the parts of Libya belonging to Cyrene, and visitors from Rome, both Jews and proselytes, ¹¹Cretans and Arabs—in our own languages we hear them speaking about God's deeds of power." ¹²All were amazed and perplexed, saying to one

another, "What does this mean?" ¹³But others sneered and said, "They are filled with new wine." ¹⁴But Peter, standing with the eleven, raised his voice and addressed them, "Men of Judea and all who live in Jerusalem, let this be known to you, and listen to what I say. ¹⁵Indeed, these are not drunk, as you suppose, for it is only nine o'clock in the morning. ¹⁶No, this is what was spoken through the prophet Joel: ¹⁷'In the last days it will be, God declares, that I will pour out my Spirit upon all flesh, and your sons and your daughters shall prophesy, and your young men shall see visions, and your old men shall dream dreams. ¹⁸Even upon my slaves, both men and women, in those days I will pour out my Spirit; and they shall prophesy. ¹⁹And I will show portents in the heaven above and signs on the earth below, blood, and fire, and smoky mist. ²⁰The sun shall be turned to darkness and the moon to blood, before the coming of the Lord's great and glorious day. ²¹Then everyone who calls on the name of the Lord shall be saved.'"

∾

A little over ten years ago I was involved in a continuing education project and had a particular question arise in the midst of the project. In due course, I came to realize that there was only one person on earth who could answer the question—literally *one* person. Putting my rudimentary computer skills to work, through a Google search I tracked down the one person on earth who knew the answer to my question. He is a retired Baptist minister who for many years pastored in London, but is from New Zealand and has retired to Australia. With the gracious help of this man's former secretary, I tracked him down in Adelaide, and over time we have become good friends via email. By the way, he did answer my question!

In the process of becoming friends, at one point he said to me in an email: "My best friend in America is a former Baptist pastor who became an Episcopal priest. Now America is such a vast country there is no possible way you would know this man, but his name is Dick Price and he lives in Asheville, North Carolina." My response: "I *do* know Dick Price. Many years ago he and I were the go-to substitutes at St. Mary's Church, Asheville, for their daily Eucharist." His response: "I'm sitting here in Adelaide simply marveling at the reality that you know Dick Price." Sometimes it really is a small world.

Well, it is and is not. In some ways the world seems smaller and smaller, with the advent of satellite communications and the internet. In some ways we *are* closer than ever. And yet... Every day, both in this country and abroad, we see distrust, division, even violence based on issues of race, ethnicity, and religion. We see the harsh realities of distrust and division every day even though people of good will know that God's will for us is unity. But sadly, division is an all-to-frequent reality. At one level, we human beings *are* closer to each other than ever. And yet how sad it is that, in reality, in so many ways we seem to be drifting farther apart. But always, always, always, as people of faith we are called to be people of hope. It is our calling to think globally and act locally for justice, for peace, and for love.

One of my mentors is a man called Carl Holladay, one of the great Bible scholars in the world. I had the privilege of serving as Dr. Holladay's research assistant at Candler School of Theology, Emory University, when I was a student there in the 1980s. In commenting on our passage he writes: "Hope is an intrinsic part of existence [in Christ]."[1] Carefully chosen words. Hope is an *intrinsic* part of existence in Christ. To be a Christian *is* to be hopeful, secure in the knowledge that love *is* stronger than hate, and that, through the power of the Spirit, change *can* come.

Initially we may think of that first Day of Pentecost in terms of chaos, particularly we Episcopalians who tend to like things done 'decently and in good order.' We may instinctively think of the 'chaos' of that first Pentecost, but upon deeper reflection the reality is that the outpouring of the Spirit fostered communication, even order, and that this resulting communication led to understanding. Thus, in the end the Day of Pentecost was not about chaos but instead represents a widely diverse gathering of people being able to communicate with and understand one another.

It was an international gathering, that festival when the Holy Spirit broke out among Jesus' followers and then spread amongst the crowd. We encounter some unfamiliar words in the Acts passage: Parthians, Medes, Elamites. It is tough duty to be the lector on Pentecost Sunday! But there is a reason for Luke giving us these tongue-twisting words. It was an *international* gathering. Pentecost had its ancient roots as an agricultural festival, but by the first century Pentecost was a celebration of the giving of the Law, and thus was an occasion for pilgrimage by Jews from all parts of the known world. Jews from throughout the diaspora made pilgrimage to Jerusalem to celebrate the festival of Pentecost. It was in this international setting that God's Holy Spirit was poured out in a way that had never been experienced before.

One of the great preachers of our time is Sam Lloyd. In a sermon for Pentecost Sunday he notes: "All of a sudden people from every corner of the world of that time found an unimaginable sense of connectedness. They experienced a oneness with each other across every barrier of race and nation."[2] A strong observation. In the 'chaos' of that first Pentecost Sunday, the gift of the Spirit brought people *together*. Lloyd goes on to state: "That Spirit is always at work, creating connection, communion, belonging."[3] That same Pentecost Spirit is always at work among us, even in the moment that is now.

On Pentecost Sunday, we do not merely commemorate one of the most important days in human history. We *do* that, but we also celebrate the *present reality* of God's Spirit at work in us. Again the words of Carl Holladay: *Hope is an intrinsic part of existence in Christ.* And the reason for that hope is the ongoing presence and power of the Spirit.

The outpouring that day was so unusual that those who were *not* in the Spirit thought that those who *were*, were drunk. Peter, in responding to this criticism, says: "it is only nine o'clock in the morning." What a wonderfully human moment. *We are not drunk*, says Peter; this is the Holy Spirit at work. Peter goes on to refer to the prophet Joel: "'In the last days it will be, God declares, that I will pour out my Spirit upon all flesh…'" Again, Pentecost was an international gathering of Jews from throughout the known world. "'I will pour out my Spirit upon *all* (emphasis added) flesh.'" Pentecost is about unity, not chaos.

We have gathered on Pentecost Sunday, 2021, still in the midst of the reality of a pandemic, though increasingly we do have reasons to be hopeful on that front. And on this Pentecost Sunday, 2021, our nation, and indeed the world, is in the midst of social stirring that is generating a time of soul searching for us all. As we gather for Pentecost 2021, we are not the same people as we were even a year ago. But, in reality, we never are. We are always changing, always evolving, always adapting—always being shaped by the events surrounding us.

One of our great preachers of recent years is Fred Craddock. In commenting on Pentecost, he writes: "When the church becomes protective and defensive, the present ceases to be God's time, and preachers become curators. The Spirit continually presses the question, What is the meaning of Jesus Christ today? and leads to answers."[4] An insightful and thought-provoking observation. What is the meaning of Jesus Christ today? Every day —consciously or unconsciously, directly or indirectly—every day we are faced with the question: What is the meaning of Jesus Christ today? To me personally? To the Church? And to the world? What is the meaning of Jesus Christ *today*?

Every year on Pentecost Sunday we renew our Baptismal Covenant as part of the liturgy. Those of us who have been in the Episcopal Church for a while are familiar with the wording of the Covenant, but to others of us it will be new. The words are haunting, if we are really open to hearing them at the deepest level.

"Will you continue in the apostles' teaching and fellowship, in the breaking of bread, and in the prayers?" "Will you persevere in resisting evil, and, whenever you fall into sin, repent and return to the Lord?" "Will you proclaim by word and example the Good News of God in Christ?" "Will you seek and serve Christ in all persons, loving your neighbor as yourself?" "Will you strive for justice and peace among all people, and respect the dignity of every human being?"[5] These are probing, challenging, haunting questions. Will *you*? Will *we*? Our answer to the questions is meant to be: "I will, with God's help."[6]

On this Pentecost Sunday, 2021, the question underlying those questions is: Will we answer by rote, or with purpose? Amen.

---

1. Carl R. Holladay, "Pentecost." *Preaching Through the Christian Year (Year B): A Comprehensive Commentary on the Lectionary* (Harrisburg, PA: Trinity Press International, 1993), 283.
2. Samuel T. Lloyd III, *Sermons From the National Cathedral: Soundings for the Journey* (Lanham, MD: Rowman & Littlefield Publishers, Inc., 2013), 321.
3. Ibid.
4. Fred B. Craddock, "Pentecost." *Preaching Through the Christian Year (Year B): A Comprehensive Commentary on the Lectionary* (Harrisburg, PA: Trinity Press International, 1993), 284.
5. *The Book of Common Prayer* (New York: The Seabury Press, 1979), 304.
6. Ibid.

17
ONE OF THE GLORY DAYS OF THE CHRISTIAN YEAR

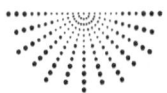

JOHN 3:1–17 • 30 MAY 2021 • TRINITY SUNDAY

¹Now there was a Pharisee named Nicodemus, a leader of the Jews. ²He came to Jesus by night and said to him, "Rabbi, we know that you are a teacher who has come from God; for no one can do these signs that you do apart from the presence of God." ³Jesus answered him, "Very truly, I tell you, no one can see the kingdom of God without being born from above." ⁴Nicodemuus said to him, "How can anyone be born after having grown old? Can one enter a second time into the mother's womb and be born?" ⁵Jesus answered, "Very truly, I tell you, no one can enter the kingdom of God without being born of water and Spirit. ⁶What is born of the flesh is flesh, and what is born of the Spirit is spirit. ⁷Do not be astonished that I said to you, 'You must be born from above.' ⁸The wind blows where it chooses, and you hear the sound of it, but you do not know where it comes from or where it goes. So it is with everyone who is born of the Spirit." ⁹Nicodemus said to him, "How can these things be?" ¹⁰Jesus answered him, "Are you a teacher of Israel, and yet you do not understand these things? ¹¹Very truly, I tell you, we speak of what we know and testify to what we

have seen; yet you do not receive our testimony. ¹²If I have told you about earthly things and you do not believe, how can you believe if I tell you about heavenly things? ¹³No one has ascended into heaven except the one who descended from heaven, the Son of Man. ¹⁴And just as Moses lifted up the serpent in the wilderness, so must the Son of Man be lifted up, ¹⁵that whoever believes in him may have eternal life. ¹⁶For God so loved the world that he gave his only Son, so that everyone who believes in him may not perish but may have eternal life. ¹⁷Indeed, God did not send the Son into the world to condemn the world, but in order that the world might be saved through him."

∼

The first church I served as an ordained minister was St. Andrew's Episcopal Church in Canton, North Carolina. I was twenty-seven years old when I was sent there. Early in my tenure I received a phone call from a representative of the Church Pension Fund who said: "Our records indicate that you are the youngest rector in the Episcopal Church. We just wanted to reach out to you and check in." It seems like yesterday that I got that phone call, but it was not. On September 1, 2020, I got a very different message from the Church Pension Fund: "Congratulations"—on thirty years of accredited service. Check in with us when you are ready to retire.

When I got to Canton as a twenty-seven-year-old the patriarch of the church was a man named Rufus Page. Rufus was a good man; there is no question about that. But he could be gruff and intimidating, and it was clear to me that his new, young minister would have to prove himself.

There came a point when Rufus asked to see me and prefaced his request with: "I have a problem I need to talk with you about." Several days passed before the two of us could get together, and if you know we well, you might imagine what I did for those several days. I turned it over and over in my head: *What have I done to upset Mr. Page?* Finally, the day of our meeting arrived. We settled into our chairs, and after exchanging pleasantries Rufus said: "Joel, here's my problem. I'm afraid that I don't fully understand the Trinity." *That* was the problem? As you might imagine, in the privacy of my mind I breathed an enormous sigh of relief. It was great to know that *I* was not the problem. Relieved of my considerable anxiety, I said to Rufus: "Well, I would be more concerned about you if you thought you *did* fully understand the Trinity."

In seminary the students take classes on preaching. The fancy seminary word for preaching class is "homiletics." Homiletics comes from a Greek word for conversation. Preaching is, after all, meant to be a kind of conversation between preacher and congregation. In homiletics class the professor walks the students through the Christian year, offering guidance on preaching in Advent, Christmas, Epiphany, etc. All these years later I remember specifically the day we covered Trinity Sunday. Our homiletics professor at Sewanee was a man named Bill Hethcock, and his sagely advice regarding Trinity Sunday was: "Trinity Sunday is an excellent day to be on vacation." Seriously, that is the exact quotation! Why would he say that regarding a Major Feast of the Church Year? Because the doctrine of the Trinity is the ultimate theological mystery.

> There is but one living and true God, everlasting, without body, parts, or passions; of infinite power, wisdom, and goodness; the Maker, and Preserver of all things both visible and invisible. And in unity of this Godhead there be three Persons, of one substance, power, and eternity; the Father, the Son, and the Holy Ghost.[1]

Our belief that we worship one God, who is made known in three distinct Persons, is a mystery that none of us can fully understand or explain from an intellectual point of view. The doctrine of the Trinity seeks to express that which is, ultimately, inexpressible.

Augustine of Hippo (354–430) is regarded as one of the great theologians in all of Christian history. Augustine wrote a treatise on the Trinity entitled *De Trinitate*. Having written such a fulsome treatment of the doctrine of the Trinity, Augustine is also remembered as having said: "If you do not believe in the Trinity you will lose your soul, but if you try to understand it you will lose your mind." That, from one of the great theological minds of all time. So, yes, we formulate theories and hold opinions about the Trinity. And yes, we sing beautiful hymns extolling the doctrine of the Trinity. And yes, theologians write their tomes on the subject of the Trinity. But, in the end, the inner workings of the Godhead are far beyond our comprehension. We take it on faith that God, in God's infinite, ultimately unknowable majesty, loved humanity enough to come to earth and take on human flesh.

It is well worth noting that Trinity Sunday is the only Major Feast of the Church Year that celebrates a doctrine. Every other Christian Feast celebrates either a person, or persons, or an event. It is only on Trinity Sunday that we celebrate a doctrine.

Dr. Hethcock's heartfelt advice was for us to take Trinity Sunday off, it being the hardest day of the year on which to preach. For most of my career, I would have agreed with him. But at this thirty-year juncture, I no longer concur. At this stage I am inclined to agree with Fleming Rutledge, one of today's great preachers, who has said in an address for Trinity Sunday that it is "one of the glory days of the Christian year."[2] Like Rutledge, I too have come to embrace Trinity Sunday as a "glory day," a day on which to celebrate the greatness of God, the infinite goodness and love of God ultimately beyond our comprehending, and yet, a God who loved humanity enough to take on human flesh and blood and live among us. "And the Word became flesh and lived among us, and we have seen his glory..."[3]

One of the great Anglican biblical scholars of all time, Charlie Moule, wrote concerning the Trinity: "That a mystery is impenetrable does not exempt the worshipper from trying to understand, and there is nothing irreverent about humble enquiry. Christian belief needs to be constantly under scrutiny."[4] For Moule, though none of us can fully understand the inner workings of the Godhead does not mean that we should not reflect deeply on the nature of God. To be sure, none of us will ever precisely understand the inner workings of the Godhead, but it is incumbent upon us to explore the Mystery, because in exploring the Mystery we are meant to be led to a greater, deeper, and, ultimately, a more humbly reverent sense of the awesomeness, in the truest sense of the word, of the nature and love of God.

It took the Christian Church over 400 years to arrive at the doctrine of the Trinity as we know it. That is longer than the United States of America has been in existence! Four centuries of theological discussion and debate. Four centuries of study, reflection, and prayer.

Cally Hammond writes in commenting on Trinity Sunday: "We have to make do without perfect clarity or monumental definitions. Instead, we must learn to work with glimpses, fragments, signs, and symbols. God does not entrust us with certainty, probably because he knows how we behave when we think we have all the right answers on our side."[5] A wise observation. God chooses to remain a Mystery, lest we think that we have gained control. God is by nature Mysterious, in the fullest sense of the word, and we are left to look for fragments, signs, symbols, and moments of deep and haunting intuition that connect us to the source of our very life.

Paul puts it this way in 1 Corinthians 13:12: "For now we see in a mirror, dimly, but then we will see face to face. Now I know only in part; then I will know fully, even as I have been fully known." Paul himself, the apostle to the Gentiles, the first great theologian of the Church, acknowledges the Mystery.

Most of us can remember when *The Da Vinci Code* was all

the rage. In this work of fiction there is one real-life contemporary theologian who is quoted, Dr. Martyn Percy. Martyn is a friend of ours and was a guest of this parish about ten years ago. He taught a Sunday School class in the Parish Hall and then preached from this pulpit. The line of Martyn's that is quoted is on the lips of Sir Leigh Teabing: "The Bible did not arrive by fax from heaven."[6] In a sermon for Trinity Sunday, Martyn Percy has said that the doctrine of the Trinity addresses: "the essence of a mystery..."[7] And: "the true Christian response to the mystery of the Trinity is not theology or philosophy, but worship."[8] In the end, the doctrine of the Trinity is not for us to understand or master, but is meant to foster humility and worship. Percy adds: "Ultimately, all the doctrine of the Trinity is trying to do is say something about the abundance of God."[9] All the theological work, over all the years—all the disputation over the fine points of doctrine—all of it is meant to lead us to appreciate the Mystery, the abundance of the incomprehensible greatness and love of God. Jesus himself puts it this way in John 10:10b: "I came that they may have life, and have it abundantly."

With all due respect to Bill Hethcock, Trinity Sunday is not an excellent day to be on vacation; it *is* one of the glory days of the Christian year, and we are gathered today to glory in the Mystery of God—Creator, Redeemer, Sustainer. The doctrine of the Trinity seeks to express that which is, ultimately, beyond expression, the breadth and depth of God's love for us. And on this glory day of the Church Year we encounter one of the most glorious verses in all of the Bible in today's Gospel lesson, John 3:16, oftentimes the first Bible verse a person learns and commits to memory, as it proclaims *the* central truth of our Christian understanding of God: "For God so loved the world that he gave his only Son, so that everyone who believes in him may not perish but may have eternal life." For Christians, the central truth, the essence of what we know about God is found in Jesus Christ, born of a woman, crucified and risen, alive and at large in the world.

Karl Barth was arguably the greatest biblical theologian of the twentieth century. His multi-volume *Church Dogmatics* is a monumental achievement in the history of Christian theology. The story goes that near the end of a long life and a prolific career of biblical scholarship, Barth was asked in a radio interview: "Given your years of experience, if you could somehow crystalize all that you have learned about God, how would you summarize the essence of the Christian faith?" He answered: "Jesus loves me, this I know, for the Bible tells me so." Amen.

---

1. *The Book of Common Prayer* (New York: The Seabury Press, 1979), 867.
2. Fleming Rutledge, *Help My Unbelief* (Grand Rapids: William B. Eerdmans Publishing Company, 2000), 28.
3. John 1:14
4. C. F. D. Moule, *Christ Alive and at Large: Unpublished Writings of C. F. D. Moule*. Canterbury Studies in Spiritual Theology. Edited and Introduced by Robert Morgan and Patrick Moule (Norwich: Canterbury Press, 2010), 175.
5. Cally Hammond, "Trinity Sunday." *Church Times*.20 May 2021. https://www.churchtimes.co.uk/articles/2021/28-may/faith/sunday-s-readings/trinity-sunday
6. Dan Brown, *The Da Vinci Code: A Novel* (New York: Doubleday, 2003), 231.
7. Martyn Percy, "Trinity Sunday." *The Bright Field: Meditations and Reflections for Ordinary Time*. Martyn Percy, Editor (Norwich: Canterbury Press, 2014), 203.
8. Ibid.
9. Ibid.

18
THE BRACING CHALLENGE OF A NEW WAY OF LIFE

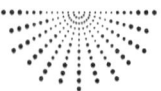

MARK 6:1–13 • 4 JULY 2021
SIXTH SUNDAY AFTER PENTECOST

¹[Jesus] came to his hometown, and his disciples followed him. ²On the sabbath he began to teach in the synagogue, and many who heard him were astounded. They said, "Where did this man get all this? What is this wisdom that has been given to him? What deeds of power are being done by his hands! ³Is not this the carpenter, the son of Mary and brother of James and Joses and Judas and Simon, and are not his sisters here with us?" And they took offense at him. ⁴Then Jesus said to them, "Prophets are not without honor, except in their hometown, and among their own kin, and in their own house." ⁵And he could do no deed of power there, except that he laid his hands on a few sick people and cured them. ⁶And he was amazed at their unbelief. Then he went about among the villages teaching. ⁷He called the twelve and began to send them out two by two, and gave them authority over the unclean spirits. ⁸He ordered them to take nothing for their journey except a staff; no bread, no bag, no money in their belts; ⁹but to wear sandals and not to put on two tunics. ¹⁰He said to them, "Wherever you enter a house, stay there until you leave the place. ¹¹If any place will not

welcome you and they refuse to hear you, as you leave, shake off the dust that is on your feet as a testimony against them." [12]So they went out and proclaimed that all should repent. [13]They cast out many demons, and anointed with oil many who were sick and cured them.

~

The French essayist Michel de Montaigne (1533–92), speaking about his hometown, observed that the greater the distance away, the greater he became. How many of us can relate to that? I can. The farther away I got from my hometown, the more respected I became.

In Mark 6:4 we read: "Prophets are not without honor, except in their hometown, and among their own kin, and in their own house." One of the more memorable of Jesus' statements. Commenting on 6:4, Kent Hughes writes: "Jesus was the victim of what all too often is a law of human relationships: familiarity breeds contempt."[1]

In preparing this sermon I thought about my hometown. There is only one place in the world where I have ever been called Joey—my hometown. Early in our dating relationship, Debbie and I were at an event in Chattanooga and, unbeknownst to either of us, a person from my hometown was there as well. In the course of the evening I noticed that this woman kept looking at me. Eventually, with the help of her husband (also from my hometown), she pieced it together, and in a room filled with Debbie's friends and colleagues, she suddenly exclaimed: "Oh my God, you're little Joey Huffstetler!" Little? A hush fell over the room. I was 35 years old at the time and had not heard "Joey" Huffstetler in nearly twenty years. If it can happen even to Jesus, then it can certainly happen to any of us. "Prophets are not without honor, except in their hometown..."

It had started off well that day. Mark tells us in 6:2: "On the sabbath he began to teach in the synagogue, and many who heard him were astounded. They said, 'Where did this man get all this? What is this wisdom that has been given to him? What deeds of power are being done by his hands!'" So far, so good. But we then read in 6:3: "'Is not this the carpenter, the son of Mary and brother of James and Joses and Judas and Simon, and are not his sisters here with us?' And they took offense at him." In his own hometown. Not all, of course, but some. *Who does he think he is? We grew up with this guy.* Again, in the words of Kent Hughes: Even Jesus could be victimized by what all too often is a law of human relationships: familiarity breeds contempt.

Mark 6:1–4 lays the groundwork for the teaching in verses 10–11. There Jesus says: "Wherever you enter a house, stay there until you leave the place. If any place will not welcome you and they refuse to hear you, as you leave, shake off the dust that is on your feet as a testimony against them." You may remember that on several occasions in the Gospels Jesus says, in effect: "Let those with ears, listen."[2] In 6:10–11, Jesus foretells that some will be open to hearing the Good News, while for others the message will fall on deaf ears. And thus his counsel: Where you are not welcomed, shake the dust off your feet and move on. Though we are wise to exercise great care in making the decision, sometimes our best course of action is to move on. From his own experience in his hometown, Jesus knew that his followers would be welcomed in some situations but not in others.

In commenting on 6:1–13, N. T. Wright observes: "There are always some who would rather stay sick than face the bracing challenge of a new way of life, a new outlook."[2] A wise observation. There are always *some* (emphasis added) who would rather stay stuck than face the bracing challenge of a new way of life, a new outlook. Of course, sometimes 'they' are *us*.

I noticed in the morning paper that one of the major cable networks is running a Harry Potter movie marathon today. Some of you will know this story, but some may not. When the original Harry Potter manuscript was presented to publishers it was rejected thirty times. Just think about being one of those thirty publishing houses today! What if *you* were one of the thirty(!) editors who passed on Harry Potter? Rejected *thirty* times. But the rest, as they say, is history. J. K. Rowling did not give up. She persevered. She shook off the dust from her feet and moved on.

Many of you know that I am a North Carolinian. Before Michael Jordan was *Michael* Jordan, he was *Mike* Jordan, a lanky, late-blooming high school basketball player in Wilmington, North Carolina. *Mike* Jordan went to Laney High School in Wilmington, and as an underclassman—a lanky, late-blooming underclassman—*Mike* Jordan was cut from his high school's varsity basketball team. Hindsight being 20/20, imagine being the coach who cut Michael Jordan! *Mike* Jordan did not make the varsity team as an underclassman, and the story goes that upon arriving back home on the day he was cut from the team his mother said to him: "You can either sulk about it, or you can prove them wrong." How is that for wisdom? You can either sulk about it, or prove them wrong. Of course, you know the rest of the story. *Mike* Jordan went on to become *Michael* Jordan, arguably the greatest basketball player of all time.

Jesus, in his unmatched wisdom, knew that there would be times when we are not heard, not understood, not welcomed. He therefore gave his disciples permission: Shake the dust off your feet and move on. Move forward. Do not give up. There will be other places, other people, other opportunities. I have used it countless times in my own life and ministry: Shake the dust off your feet, and move on.

Today is July the Fourth. Independence Day falls on a Sunday this year. Independence Day is recognized by the Episcopal Church as a Major Feast Day. In the Episcopal Church, Independence Day is accorded the same status as that of Thanksgiving Day. Our Church recognizes that, from a spiritual perspective, Independence Day is just as theologically grounded as is Thanksgiving Day. Independence Day is not only a national holiday, as important as that is to us. The Declaration of Independence was framed (no pun intended) in spiritual terms. And though we continue to struggle to this day to live up to its ideals, the vision for this country was and is firmly grounded in spiritual aspirations. And so today, in place of the usual Prayers of the People we will offer prayers of thanksgiving for our national life.

In a few moments we will pray: "We thank you for the men and women who have made this country strong. They are models for us, though we often fall short of them."[3] Independence Day is a time to remember all those who have gone before us, and those who are with us now, who remind us of the ideals for which this country strives. And we will pray: "Help us, O Lord, to finish the good work here begun. Strengthen our efforts to blot out ignorance and prejudice, and to abolish poverty and crime. And hasten the day when all our people, with many voices in one united chorus, will glorify your holy Name."[4]

When we step back from the trees to see the forest, we are reminded that Independence Day is indeed as deeply grounded in Judeo-Christian values as is Thanksgiving Day. And the question before us all on this and every July the Fourth is: Do we see, embrace, and commit ourselves to facing the challenges still before us in forming a more perfect Union? Amen.

---

1. R. Kent Hughes, *Mark: Jesus, Servant and Savior.* Preaching the Word. R. Kent Hughes, Editor (Wheaton, IL: Crossway, 2015), 130.
2. N. T. Wright, *Mark for Everyone* (London: Society for Promoting Christian Knowledge, 2001), 69.
3. *The Book of Common Prayer* (New York: The Seabury Press, 1979), 839.
4. *Ibid.*

19

A STRONG SENSE OF SELF

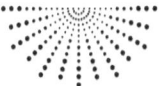

MARK 6:14–29 • 11 JULY 2021
SEVENTH SUNDAY AFTER PENTECOST

¹⁴King Herod heard of [Jesus and his disciples], for Jesus' name had become known. Some were saying, "John the Baptizer has been raised from the dead; and for this reason these powers are at work in him." ¹⁵But others said, "It is Elijah." And others said, "It is a prophet, like one of the prophets of old." ¹⁶But when Herod heard of it, he said, "John, whom I beheaded, has been raised." ¹⁷For Herod himself had sent men who arrested John, bound him, and put him in prison on account of Herodias, his brother Philip's wife, because Herod had married her. ¹⁸For John had been telling Herod, "It is not lawful for you to have your brother's wife." ¹⁹And Herodias had a grudge against him, and wanted to kill him. But she could not, ²⁰for Herod feared John, knowing that he was a righteous and holy man, and he protected him. When he heard him, he was greatly perplexed; and yet he liked to listen to him. ²¹But an opportunity came when Herod on his birthday gave a banquet for his courtiers and officers and for the leaders of Galilee. ²²When his daughter Herodias came in and danced, she pleased Herod and his guests; and the king said to the girl, "Ask me for whatever you wish, and I

will give it." ²³And he solemnly swore to her, "Whatever you ask me, I will give you, even half of my kingdom." ²⁴She went out and said to her mother, "What should I ask for?" She replied, "The head of John the baptizer. ²⁵Immediately she rushed back to the king and requested, "I want you to give me at once the head of John the Baptist on a platter." ²⁶The king was deeply grieved; yet out of regard for his oaths and for the guests, he did not want to refuse her. ²⁷Immediately the king sent a soldier of the guard with orders to bring John's head. He went and beheaded him in the prison, ²⁸brought his head on a platter, and gave it to the girl. Then the girl gave it to her mother. ²⁹When his disciples heard about it, they came and took his body, and laid it in a tomb."

In commenting on this scene that recounts the death of John the Baptist, N. T. Wright observes: "It's sordid, shabby and shameful—exactly the sort of thing that everybody likes to hear, however much they pretend otherwise."¹ And in a sermon on our passage Mark Oakley asks: "This may be an ancient story but was one ever more fresh?"² It does have it all: royalty, sensuality, blood, guilt, revenge. To be sure, this story recounts both moral weakness and moral courage. In the court of Herod we see abuse of power and scandal. In John the Baptist we see integrity.

In Matthew 11:11a Jesus is recorded as saying: "Truly I tell you, among those born of women no one has arisen greater than John the Baptist..." We know that John the Baptist had a strong personality, a strong sense of self. We know that he had a deep faith, and we know that he is a figure of lasting historical significance. And yet we also remember about John the Baptist that he was humble. John was content to be the forerunner of the Messiah and not the center of attention. For all his obvious charisma, and for all his strong personality, John the Baptist was, in the end, content to be the messenger, secure in the knowledge that his role was to prepare the way for the Messiah and not to be the Messiah himself. And thus John the Baptist, for all his obvious strength of character, is an iconic role model of a healthy, a proper sense of humility.

When Debbie was in college she worked for a man who was the number two administrator of her college, second only to the president. This man had been in that position for years, and, predictably, people frequently would ask him: "Don't you want to move up? Wouldn't you like to be president of a college somewhere?" And every time he was asked, his response was: "No, I am a number one number two man." His stance is one of the best and most memorable ways to frame the subject of humility I have ever encountered: *I'm a number one number two man.* Sometimes we are wise to stay in our lane.

Robert Gates is the only secretary of defense in our nation's history to have served both a Republican and a Democrat administration. Bob Gates is a great source of ideas and reflections on leadership. He has written an outstanding book on leadership, and in the book Gates makes the point that we need strong leaders at every level of society. Here is a man who has served at the highest levels of government, he has been the president of two major universities, and yet Gates has the awareness, the humility, to realize that we need strong capable leaders at every level. And he is specific; we need strong city council members, strong county officials. He even says that we need strong local pastors and capable Sunday School teachers. His is a discerning take on leadership. We cannot allow ourselves to think of leadership in terms of everyone working to make their way to the top. We need outstanding people at every level of society. And thus we need people to realize that there is good, important, *vital* work to be done at every level of society, beginning at the local level.

I am a number one number two man. John the Baptist had this realization and was secure and content in his calling, embracing the role for which he was born rather than always thinking: What else should I be doing?

John the Baptist was a number two man, but he was a number one at it, so much so that our passage makes clear in verse 29 that John had his own disciples, his own followers. John the Baptist had earned the deepest respect of Jesus, and he even had the respect of Herod. Notice in 6:19–20a: "And Herodias had a grudge against him, and wanted to kill him. But she could not, for Herod feared John, knowing that he was a righteous and holy man, and he protected him." Herod wanted to protect John because he had a basic respect for him. In 6:20b we read: "When he heard him, he was greatly perplexed; and yet he liked to listen to him." John the Baptist had earned Herod's respect. But...

Be careful what you ask for. And what you promise! We read in 6:26: "The king was deeply grieved; yet out of regard for his oaths and for the guests, he did not want to refuse [Herodias' daughter]." Herod boxed himself in through his hasty, unreflective promise. Mark notes that Herod was "deeply grieved." There is only one other time in the Gospel of Mark when the term "deeply grieved" is used—in the Garden of Gethsemane. Jesus says in 14:34–35: "'I am deeply grieved, even to death; remain here, and keep awake.' And going a little farther, he threw himself on the ground and prayed that, if it were possible, the hour might pass from him." The same level of emotion Jesus shows in the Garden of Gethsemane, Herod shows for his decision regarding John the Baptist.

In commenting on our passage, Kent Hughes notes: "[John the Baptist] was a man of conscience and moral courage. One day he would lose his head, but not his conscience."[3] What a succinct and insightful testimony to the character and the courage of John the Baptist. When put to the ultimate test, John the Baptist had the courage of his convictions.

Mark 6:14–29 is the only passage in the Gospel of Mark that is not specifically about Jesus. Every other passage in the Gospel of Mark *is* specifically about Jesus, but John the Baptist was of such lasting importance that Mark saw fit to record how John met his death. While our passage is not specifically about Jesus, we know that everything John did was on behalf of Jesus. Ultimately even this passage, which is specifically about John, leads us back to the one to whom John pointed—Jesus.

In the aforementioned sermon on our passage, Mark Oakley writes: "[Jesus] didn't ask for admirers, he asked for disciples."[4] A crisp and insightful observation. When we hear "disciple" we may instinctively think "follower," and, to be sure, a disciple is a follower. But in the Greek the primary definition of "disciple" is "learner." Learner carries with it at least a slightly more active connotation than "follower." Yes, disciples follow, but they follow in order to learn, and thus Oakley's point: Jesus was not looking for *admirers*, he was looking for *disciples*. Oakley goes on to say: "We are not to be, please God, Facebook friends of Jesus, but apprentices, ready to follow even to the darkest, frightening, alone places that truth and fidelity will take us and that John the Baptist blessed by his presence 2,000 years ago."[5] Even today, Jesus is not looking for Facebook friends! He is not looking for casual admirers, but *apprentices—learners*—people who take the essence of his message and apply it in their daily living. The distinction of the nuanced difference between follower and learner can help us to remember that to follow Christ is meant to be an active, lifetime journey of learning more and more what it means to look to Christ for guidance in every life situation.

Two millennia after the event recorded in our passage, Herod Antipas is remembered by history as a petty tyrant, a king in name only. In the end, Herod Antipas was nothing but a puppet of the Roman government. But in John the Baptist we see true strength of character. We see integrity. And in John the Baptist we see moral courage that was put to the ultimate test. We aspire to be like Christ, and that is as it should be. But we can also aspire to be like John the Baptist. John the Baptist was as human as we are, flesh and blood just like us, and he remains an important role model for us. He had a humble spirit, and yet a strong sense of self

—and vocational purpose. And when *the* moment of crisis presented itself, John showed the depth and the strength of his moral character.

Every day we face choice after choice. And the choice is always before us—to do what we know to be right. Amen.

---

1. N. T. Wright, *Mark for Everyone* (London: Society for Promoting Christian Knowledge, 2001), 75.
2. Mark Oakley, *By Way of the Heart: The Seasons of Faith* (Norwich: Canterbury Press, 2019), 10.
3. R. Kent Hughes, *Mark: Jesus, Servant and Savior.* Preaching the Word. R. Kent Hughes, Editor (Wheaton, IL: Crossway, 2015), 137.
4. Oakley, 11.
5. *Ibid.*

20
COMPASSION

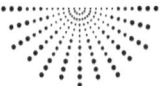

MARK 6:30–34, 53–56 • 18 JULY 2021
EIGHTH SUNDAY AFTER PENTECOST

³⁰The apostles gathered around Jesus, and told him all that they had done and taught. ³¹He said to them, "Come away to a deserted place all by yourselves and rest a while." For many were coming and going, and they had no leisure even to eat. ³²And they went away in the boat to a deserted place by themselves. ³³Now many saw them going and recognized them, and they hurried there on foot from all the towns and arrived ahead of them. ³⁴As he went ashore, he saw a great crowd; and he had compassion for them, because they were like sheep without a shepherd; and he began to teach them many things. ⁵³When they had crossed over, they came to land at Gennesaret and moored the boat. ⁵⁴When they got out of the boat, people at once recognized him, ⁵⁵and rushed about that whole region and began to bring the sick on mats to wherever they heard he was. ⁵⁶And wherever he went, into villages or cities or farms, they laid the sick in the marketplaces, and begged him that they might touch even the fringe of his cloak; and all who touched it were healed.

One of the expectations that comes along with being an active parish priest in a diocese is attendance at an annual clergy conference—continuing education for clergy. Extroverts love clergy conferences! They love seeing their friends. They thrive on the energy and interaction of the gathered clergy. And they love *sharing* with one another.

Introverts have a markedly different experience at clergy conferences. In years past, when I was younger in ministry, in the midst of seemingly interminable clergy conference sessions I would look at the door longing to bolt right through it. A couple of years ago I reached the point in my career where I now *am* that clergy who heads for the exit when the facilitator announces excitedly: "Now, let's break into small groups so that we can share in more detail what we're experiencing and how we are feeling." Age has its privileges.

Happily, on occasion there is an exception, and something of lasting value comes out of a clergy conference session. For me, there was one such conference well over a decade ago. We were meeting in Gatlinburg, Tennessee, and the guest speaker was talking in general terms about the demands of parish ministry, and how clergy never know from one day to the next where we will be or who will call on us. I have a specific memory of her presentation being quite engaging and worthwhile. That said, I only remember one specific sentence from the presentation, but that one sentence I will remember forever: "What we all have to remember is that the interruptions *are* the job." Nailed it. For parish clergy the interruptions are *not* interruptions. The interruptions *are* the job. A one-liner every parish minister should hear, and accept.

In the Gospels Jesus clearly understands the need for regular, intentional times of rest. We see numerous moments in the Gospels when Jesus clearly understands the need for Sabbath. We all need a break at regular intervals—even Jesus! It is essential, for the good of all concerned that spiritual leaders are disciplined about taking time for rest and renewal. But, of all people, Jesus also knew that the 'interruptions' *are* the job.

We see an example of this in Mark 6:30–34, 53–56. Here is the context of our passage. The disciples have just returned from having been sent out by Jesus for the first time to do ministry in his name. He sent them out two by two, and in our passage the disciples have come back from that first time out on their own. Jesus knows that they need to rest, and they need time to reflect. And thus he says in 6:31a: "Come away to a deserted place all by yourselves and rest a while." Now let us think about life in first-century Palestine. Upon hearing that Jesus was nearby, the crowds could not wait and see a summary of his activities on the evening news. They could not wait and read about it in the next morning's newspaper. Nor could they simply Google it. In Jesus' day, when people heard that he was in the area they would have flocked—they would have dropped what they were doing and rushed to see him. Perhaps it would be their only opportunity to see him, to hear him, and yes, as our passage indicates, to touch him in their desperate desire for healing.

Of all people, Jesus knew full well that the interruptions are the job. Our passage makes this clear. The verse that shows it most clearly is Mark 6:34: "As he went ashore [intending to rest], he saw a great crowd; and he had compassion for them, because they were like sheep without a shepherd…" Much Christian imagery and symbolism has to do with sheep and shepherds. Jesus saw that those in the crowd, in their neediness, were like sheep without a shepherd. And his best laid plans for rest and reflection notwithstanding, Jesus saw their need and responded with compassion.

A word about the Greek for "compassion." To put it in the most polite terms possible, the Greek word for "compassion" in the New Testament makes reference to our innards—our viscera. To 'feel' *compassion* in biblical Greek is to be moved in one's *innermost* self. The Greek for compassion in 6:34 refers literally to our internal organs. Such is the depth of compassion that Jesus shows, and that level of compassion is what we are meant to emulate. In our lexicon we may refer to something being *gut-wrenching*. Notice the connection to 6:34. When something devastating has happened we may say: "I feel like I've been punched in the stomach." What hurts when we have been punched in the stomach? Our internal organs. Our own understanding in contemporary English of compassion is linked with the Greek of 6:34. *Compassion* in the New Testament comes from the core of our innermost being, and it is this level of compassion that Jesus offered to those in need. There are nine references in the New Testament to this level of compassion—the level of viscera—and all nine references are in regard to Jesus himself. Jesus was moved to his core in responding to people in need.

"As he went ashore, he saw a great crowd; and he had compassion for them, because they were like sheep without a shepherd..." With all due respect to Mark, it is Matthew's account of this episode that most of us remember. In recounting the same event, Matthew words it this way in 9:36: "When he saw the crowds, he had compassion for them, because they were harassed and helpless, like sheep without a shepherd." Mark and Matthew are clearly presenting the same event, but Matthew adds just that little extra touch. The crowds were *harassed and helpless,* and Jesus could not do other than respond to them with deep compassion.

Now back to Mark. In commenting on the usage of compassion in 6:34 James A. Brooks writes: "[Compassion] suggests something more than mere pity; it suggests actual help."[1] A crucial point regarding Jesus' understanding of compassion. As important as an initial emotional reaction to someone in need is, that emotional response is meant to be followed, whenever possible, by action. Yes, we may *feel* deeply for someone in need, or for a situation involving numbers of people, but after that initial *feeling* and awareness the question is: "What can I do?" Or,

"What can *we* do?" To be sure, whenever possible our response is meant to be more than "thoughts and prayers."

If we look up "compassion" in an English dictionary, the primary definition is "sympathetic consciousness of others' distress together with a desire to alleviate it..."[2] So yes, Christian compassion starts with a feeling, a gut-level reaction, but then that initial reaction is meant to be followed by a concrete response which reflects the love of Christ.

Mark 6:34 in its entirety: "As he went ashore, he saw a great crowd; and he had compassion for them, because they were like sheep without a shepherd; and he began to teach them many things." Here we see the desired balance: an initial emotional response followed by concrete, practical action. The 'harassed and helpless' people who crowded around Jesus did not just need sympathy. They needed action. Yes, thoughts and prayers, but then *action*. Jesus models for us the desired two-pronged understanding of compassion.

In our modern lexicon we recognize the phrase: "I feel your pain." Sometimes we say it casually, even playfully. But there are times when those words are uttered in all seriousness: I *feel* your pain. This is the beginning of a true biblical understanding of compassion.

In commenting on 6:34 Cally Hammond writes: "True compassion is something that we feel in our *inmost* (emphasis added) selves, where our hearts beat faster and our stomach *churns* (emphasis added) as we react to the needs of others."[3] In the spirit of true biblical compassion we can say in utter seriousness: I *feel* your pain.

At this point my mind takes me to the Baptismal Covenant in the Book of Common Prayer. As we proceed through the Covenant the three final questions stop us in our tracks, if we have 'ears to hear.' Those of you familiar with the Baptismal Covenant will probably be able to finish these questions in your own mind as I verbalize them. "Will you proclaim by word and example the Good News of God in Christ?"[4] And then: "Will you seek and serve Christ in all persons, loving your neighbor as yourself?"[5] And then the Covenant confronts us with the question: "Will you *strive* (emphasis added) for justice and peace among all people, and respect the dignity of every human being?"[6] Three probing, haunting questions which seek to elicit a promise of action. Our response to the questions is meant to be: "I will, with God's help."[7] I will *do* these things with God's help. Another way to frame our response might be: I will, in word *and* deed.

I have long since been at peace with the reality that in pastoral ministry the interruptions *are* the job, they are not interruptions. If I had a dollar for every time I have heard over the course of thirty years in parish ministry: "I know that it's your day off, but..."

Here is an instructive and inspiring contemporary reflection on compassion. Though not a one-liner, these words hit me like a ton of bricks when I first encountered them, and they have stuck with me ever since. The quotation is from Sam Keen:

> In the spiritual journey, the compass unfailingly points toward compassion. This spiritual compass is the equivalent of the satellite Global Position[ing] System... Inscribe this single word on your heart—"compassion." Whenever you are confused, keep heading in the direction that leads toward deepening your love and care for all living beings, including yourself, and you will never stray far from the path to fulfillment.[8]

Amen.

---

1. James A. Brooks, *The New American Commentary: Mark*. Volume 23. David S. Dockery, General Editor (Nashville: B & H Publishing Group, 1991), 108.
2. *Webster's Ninth New Collegiate Dictionary* (Springfield, MA: Merriam-Webster Inc., Publishers, 1987), 268.
3. Cally Hammond, "7th Sunday after Trinity." *Church Times.* 08 July 2021.

https://www.churchtimes.co.uk/articles/2021/16-july/faith/sunday-s-readings/7th-sunday-after-trinity

4. *The Book of Common Prayer* (New York: The Seabury Press, 1979), 305.
5. *Ibid.*
6. *Ibid.*
7. *Ibid.*
8. Sam Keen, *Hymns to an Unknown God: Awakening the Spirit in Everyday Life* (New York: Bantam Books, 1994), 59.

21

ONE PHONE CALL AWAY

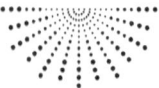

EPHESIANS 3:14–21 • 25 JULY 2021
NINTH SUNDAY AFTER PENTECOST

¹⁴For this reason I bow my knees before the Father, ¹⁵from whom every family in heaven and on earth takes its name. ¹⁶I pray that, according to the riches of his glory, he may grant that you may be strengthened in your inner being with power through his Spirit, ¹⁷and that Christ may dwell in your hearts through faith, as you are being rooted and grounded in love. ¹⁸I pray that you may have the power to comprehend, with all the saints, what is the breadth and length and height and depth, ¹⁹and to know the love of Christ that surpasses knowledge, so that you may be filled with all the fullness of God. ²⁰Now to him who by the power at work within us is able to accomplish abundantly far more than all we can ask or imagine, ²¹to him be glory in the church and in Christ Jesus to all generations, forever and ever. Amen.

~

"For this reason I bow my knees before the Father, from whom every family in heaven and on earth takes its name." "For this reason..." What reason? We need only look back a couple of verses to find the answer. In Ephesians 3:11–12 we read: "This was in accordance with the eternal purpose that he has carried out in Christ Jesus our Lord, in whom we have access to God in boldness and confidence through faith in him." Our passage is a prayer of thanksgiving for the gift of Jesus Christ to us.

Karl Barth is arguably the most influential biblical theologian of the twentieth century. Early in his career, Barth lectured on the Epistle to the Ephesians and offered this comment on our passage: "Here, at the conclusion of chapter 3, we reach the summit of the entire letter."[1] Much more recently, C. Leslie Mitton has written of 3:14–21: "This short paragraph is one of the gems of the [New Testament]."[2]

We have before us one of the glorious passages in all of the New Testament. Just a quick note on the Greek text. In it 3:11–19 forms one continuous sentence and constitutes a continuous flow of thought. Thus what we have in 3:11–21 is an outpouring of praise for the depth and riches of God's love made known to us most fully in Jesus Christ.

"For this reason I bow my knees before the Father..." The primary posture for prayer in the biblical era was standing. Most people when they prayed stood, with their arms opened. To kneel was not unprecedented, but the primary posture for prayer was standing, and thus what is happening here is that Paul is trying to portray a particular moment of reverence, a moment of especially deep respect for the extravagance of the love of God: *I bow my knees before the Father...*

Standing may well have been the predominant posture for prayer in biblical times but, again, kneeling was not unprecedented. We may remember that pivotal moment in Jesus' life and ministry recorded for us in Luke 22:41–42, Jesus in the Garden of Gethsemane. Luke writes: "Then he withdrew from them about a stone's throw, knelt down, and prayed, 'Father, if you are willing, remove this cup from me, yet, not my will but yours be done.'" Here we see Jesus kneeling in a particularly deep, prayerful spirit.

We see that same type of deep spiritual reverence mirrored in our passage.

In looking both at the Ephesians passage and the Luke passage we see both Jesus and Paul kneeling in an intimate relationship of trust with God. Right before the pandemic, which seems like ages ago, Debbie and I and a number of you were at a fundraiser for the Friends of the Library Association. It was held at Cleveland Golf and Country Club, and Karen Mills was the keynote speaker. Karen Mills is a native of Bradley County, and many of you will know her. In 1976 she hit *the* shot in the state tournament that brought a state championship here, which makes her 'royalty' in this community. These days, Karen Mills is a touring comedienne and motivational speaker. Karen Mills does 'clean' comedy—edgy, but clean. On the night, she gave a wonderful performance. She was funny! But there came a time in the performance when the mood shifted. Karen Mills is a cancer survivor, and in the middle of her otherwise hilarious act she shifted gears, got serious, and talked to us about surviving cancer and what the journey for her was like. In doing so, she was offering her support to those facing a similar struggle. A one-liner from that part of her program has stuck with me to this day. I can remember her words exactly: "We're all just one phone call away from being on our knees." One sentence that says so much: We're *all* just one phone call away from being on our knees.

I will not go into too much detail, but during the last month or so Debbie and I have had our own experience that very nearly brought us to our knees. We got one of 'those' phone calls. In recent weeks we have had *that* moment when suddenly everything comes into focus. In such moments we remember what really matters, and realize in a deeper way what does not. We never know, any of us, when *that* moment will come. We do not know from one moment to the next when everything might change. What Paul is saying in this beautifully poetic passage is that when *that* moment does come, we do not have to experience it alone. When that moment comes, when everything changes and suddenly survival itself is our only goal—in that moment, whatever the challenge, we do not have to face it alone. *I bow my knees before the Father...*

In Jesus Christ, God's love was embodied, enfleshed—incarnate. And the normative posture for prayer notwithstanding, Paul is driven to his knees in thanking God for the gift of Jesus Christ.

The Common English Bible translates 3:14–15: "This is why I kneel before the Father. Every ethnic group in heaven or on earth is recognized by him." One of the foundational themes of Ephesians is the unity of humanity. Paul's vision is for Jews and Gentiles alike to come to see each other as sisters and brothers in Christ. To be sure, the language in the New Revised Standard Version is beautiful in its own right: "from whom every family in heaven and on earth takes its name." But the Common English Bible translates it even more dynamically: "Every ethnic group in heaven or on earth is recognized by him."

I bow my knees before the Father... Mitton notes: "homage and prayer are inseparable."[3] It is important for us to remember that prayer is not only about asking. A part of prayer is homage. When we look up the word 'homage' in an English dictionary its definition includes, "reverential regard: respect."[4] When we kneel for prayer, or even when we stand, we do so to adore the very Spirit to whom we are praying. *Homage and prayer are inseparable.* Paul's love of God in Christ is so deep that he bows his knees in homage, out of the deepest respect and with the most profound gratitude for the love of God in Christ.

We then come to 3:18–19: "I pray that you may have the power to comprehend, with all the saints, what is the breadth and length and height and depth, and to know the love of Christ that surpasses knowledge, so that you may be filled with all the fullness of God." Again, in the Greek text the majority of 3:14–21 is one long sentence, an outpouring of passionate spiritual reflection. Paul is saying to his audience that, in Jesus Christ, Christians are in receipt of the most precious gift the world has ever known. Paul urges us not to allow the stresses and strains of life to cause us to lose sight of the precious gift of the risen Christ's love and Spirit.

There is a similar passage in another of Paul's letters. Romans offers us the most systematic, comprehensive theology that we get from Paul. Paul did not found the church in Rome, and thus he had to introduce himself, and his letter to them outlines, in the most comprehensive and mature form we have, the ideas that Paul found most important to the Christian experience. For example, we read in Romans 8:37–39:

> No, in all these things we are more than conquerors through him who loved us. For I am convinced that neither death, nor life, nor angels, nor rulers, nor things present, nor things to come, nor powers, nor height, nor depth, nor anything else in all creation, will be able to separate us from the love of God in Christ Jesus our Lord.

The most precious gift we have, says Paul, is the sure knowledge of the love of God—come what may—and that humanity's knowledge of that love is no longer limited to the realm of ideas. The love that surpasses human understanding was and is now embodied forever in Jesus of Nazareth—Christ risen and active, alive and at large in the world.

In the Greco-Roman world, the pinnacle of human achievement was thought to be the attainment of wisdom. The most important path one could pursue in life was to be wise. Paul counters that cultural assumption. For Paul, the pinnacle of human achievement is to know love. 1 Corinthians 13:

> [1]If I speak in the tongues of mortals and of angels, but do not have love, I am a noisy gong or a clanging cymbal. And if I have prophetic powers, and understand all mysteries and all knowledge, and I have all faith, so as to remove mountains, but do not have love, I am nothing. If I give away all my possessions, and if I hand over my body so that I may boast, but do not have love, I

gain nothing. Love is patient; love is kind; love is not envious or boastful or arrogant or rude. It does not insist on its own way; it is not irritable or resentful; it does not rejoice in wrongdoing, but rejoices in the truth. It bears all things, believes all things, hopes all things, endures all things. Love never ends. But as for prophecies, they will come to an end; as for tongues, they will cease; as for knowledge, it will come to an end. For we know only in part, and we prophesy in part; but when the complete comes, the partial will come to an end. When I was a child, I spoke like a child, I thought like a child, I reasoned like a child; when I became an adult, I put an end to childish ways. For now we see in a mirror, dimly, but then we will see face to face. Now I know only in part; then I will know fully, even as I have been fully known. And now faith, hope and love abide, these three; and the greatest of these is love.

Amen.

---

1. Karl Barth, *The Epistle to the Ephesians*. R. David Nelson, Editor. Ross M. Wright, Translator (Grand Rapids: Baker Academic, 2017), 143.
2. C. Leslie Mitton, *Ephesians*. The New Century Bible Commentary. Ronald E. Clements and Matthew Black, General Editors (Grand Rapids: William B. Eerdmans Publishing Company, 1973), 129.
3. *Ibid.*, 130.
4. *Webster's Ninth New Collegiate Dictionary* (Springfield, MA: Merriam-Webster Inc., Publishers, 1987), 577.

22

THE MINISTERS—
ALL OF THE PEOPLE

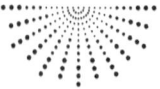

EPHESIANS 4:1–16 • 1 AUGUST 2021
TENTH SUNDAY AFTER PENTECOST

¹I therefore, the prisoner in the Lord, beg you to lead a life worthy of the calling to which you have been called, ²with all humility and gentleness, with patience, bearing with one another in love, ³making every effort to maintain the unity of the Spirit in the bond of peace. ⁴There is one body and one Spirit, just as you were called to the one hope of your calling, ⁵one Lord, one faith, one baptism, ⁶one God and Father of all, who is above all and through all and in all. ⁷But each of us was given grace according to the measure of Christ's gift. ⁸Therefore it is said, "When he ascended on high he made captivity itself a captive; he gave gifts to his people." ⁹(When it says, "He ascended," what does it mean but that he had also descended into the lower parts of the earth? ¹⁰He who descended is the same one who ascended far above all the heavens, so that he might fill all things.) ¹¹The gifts he gave were that some would be apostles, some prophets, some evangelists, some pastors and teachers, ¹²to equip the saints for the work of ministry, for building up the body of Christ, ¹³until all of us come to the unity of the faith and of the knowledge of the Son of God, to maturity, to the measure of the full

stature of Christ. ¹⁴We must no longer be children, tossed to and fro and blown about by every wind of doctrine, by people's trickery, by their craftiness in deceitful scheming. ¹⁵But speaking the truth in love, we must grow up in every way into him who is the head, into Christ, ¹⁶from whom the whole body, joined and knit together by every ligament with which it is equipped, as each part is working properly, promotes the body's growth in building itself up in love.

~

I was well into my college years before I knew anything about the Episcopal Church. The Episcopal congregation in my hometown was so small that I did not even know it existed. It turns out that I had some friends who went there, but they never talked about their church. So I was in college before the Episcopal Church appeared on my radar.

During my second semester at Elon, Dr. Robert Delp invited me to be his student assistant. Bob Delp had served as a pastor in Hagerstown, Maryland for seven years, after which he returned to graduate school and a life in academia, though he remained an ordained minister for the rest of his life. We grew close over time, and he and I would have engaging conversations regarding my future vocation. As is the case with many of us, when I was in college, I was not yet clear as to what my life's work would be. But by then I did know a couple of things about myself. One, I did not want to work with my hands. And two, I hated math. Law school was an option, but I could never generate any real enthusiasm for the prospect of practicing law. And I actively considered a career in the military, but could not generate any real enthusiasm for ROTC!

I tell you all of that to say this: From my junior year in college I can remember where in the hallway we were standing one afternoon outside Bob Delp's office talking about my lack of vocational clarity when he said: "You'll be an Episcopal priest someday." Those were his exact words: *You'll be an Episcopal priest someday.* I laughed and said: "Well, it would help if I were an Episcopalian." After all, how can a non-Episcopalian be an Episcopal priest? So there I was, laughing and thinking: What a strange thing to say. Dr. Delp allowed my laughter to subside, and then said: "You'll be an Episcopal priest someday." Somehow, he knew.

It ended up that I went to graduate school at Candler School of Theology, Emory University to pursue a Master of Theological Studies degree in preparation for PhD work. Upon arrival in Atlanta I visited several churches of different denominations on Sundays, but nothing clicked. Deep into my first semester, there came an evening when a classmate, a second-career student named Lora Groton, asked me: "Do you go to church anywhere?" The context of this brief conversation is important. There I was, a full-time graduate student in *theology*, and the question was: Do you go to church anywhere? My response: "I *have* visited some churches. I've looked around. But no, I don't really go to church anywhere." To which she responded: "Well, I think you might like St. Philip's Episcopal Cathedral." There followed a gracious invitation, and having no real reason to decline it, I said: "Yes, I'll meet you there sometime." And I did, the very next Sunday. And that is the day everything began to change for me. One hour—one service—after which I knew that I had found what I was looking for. In that one hour, it clicked, and everything began falling into place for me regarding church life. And all these years later, here I am.

The most lasting memory I have from my initial visit to St. Philip's is the bulletin. Strange, but true. On that first visit to an Episcopal Church I noticed that the masthead had listed all the major players: the bishop, the cathedral clergy, the musicians, educators, administrators, housekeeping staff, etc. But at the bottom of all the usual suspects there was something I had never seen before in all the years I had been in church: "The Ministers—All of the People." The *Ministers—All* of the people. From that initial visit I began to recognize that the Episcopal Church regarded everyone, not just the clergy, as ministers. I had been in church my entire life but had never encountered that idea, that all of the people, not just the clergy, are ministers. This is without doubt the strongest memory of my first encounter with the Episcopal Church: The Ministers—All of the People.

We have a section in our Prayer Book titled "The Catechism," and in a sub-section titled, "The Ministry," the first question is: "Who are the ministers of the Church?" And the answer is: "The ministers of the Church are lay persons, bishops, priests, and deacons."[1] There it is in black and white. In the Episcopal Church there are *four* orders of ministry, not three, the first order of ministry being lay persons.

The second question is: "What is the ministry of the laity?" So, here is your job description. "The ministry of lay persons is to represent Christ and his Church; to bear witness to him wherever they may be; and, according to the gifts given them, to carry on Christ's work of reconciliation in the world; and to take their place in the life, worship, and governance of the Church."[2] Pretty important work, is it not? To represent Christ wherever you are. To carry on the work of reconciliation that Christ himself came to offer. Just think for a moment of all the many and varied gifts and talents for ministry to be found in this one parish church. The laity is the *first* order of ministry.

Dr. Don Armentrout taught church history at Sewanee for decades. Don was an eccentric in many ways, was one of the funniest people I have ever known, and was an exceptionally dedicated member of the seminary faculty. All these years later I can well remember Don teaching us about the four orders of ministry, and of the laity's foundational importance in the life of the Church. As Don pointed out, we *all* start out as laity. I have a clear memory of one particular class session during which Don leaned out over the lectern and said to us seminarians—with a knowing wink—"Always remember, there are more of *them* than there are of you." There are more of *them* (laity) than there are of *you* (clergy). Classic Don Armentrout. And classic teaching of the Episcopal Church.

Where does this idea come from, that we all are ministers, that we all have gifts and talents for ministry. At least in part it comes from Ephesians 4:1–16. In verses 11–12 we read: "The gifts [Christ] gave were that some would be apostles, some prophets, some evangelists, some pastors and teachers," and here is the good part, "to equip the saints for the work of ministry, for building up the body of Christ..." And *you* are the saints. The word for "saint" in biblical Greek means "set apart." It does not carry with it a connotation of moral or ethical perfection. Of course, we all sin and fall short of the glory of God. In its New Testament context, to be a saint is to be set apart, to be called to and equipped for ministry in the name of Christ. So 'they' are us. The Episcopal Church's teaching that all parishioners are ministers of the Gospel is built in no small measure on our passage.

To be sure, this list of gifts is not comprehensive. It is not exhaustive. Paul gives us another such list in Romans 12, and yet another in 1 Corinthians 12, and they are not comprehensive or exhaustive either. When we stop and think about it, we realize that there are as many different potential ministries as there are people. In all our diversity, we are called to share our varied gifts for the common good in building up the body of Christ.

There is a particularly instructive passage in Mark 10 in which Jesus is schooling his disciples on remaining humble. At this point in the narrative, the disciples have been around Jesus long enough to have started looking for a pecking order as to who is closest to the throne. Jesus calls an immediate and unambiguous halt to it, reminding them in no uncertain terms that following him is about servanthood—not power. To follow Jesus means to be humble. And there comes that seminal moment in 10:45 when Jesus says of himself: "For the Son of Man came not to be served but to serve, and to give his life a ransom for many." The idea that we all are called to ministry is grounded in Jesus' own understanding that he himself was a servant.

In commenting on our passage Cally Hammond writes: "The Christian faith may be named after the risen Christ, but it is not hero worship."[3] A strong point. To be a Christian is not simply to admire the heroic figure of Jesus. Christianity is not hero worship—it is a call to action. Remember: "The gifts he gave were that some would be apostles, some prophets, some evangelists, some pastors and teachers, to equip the saints for the work of ministry, for building up the body of Christ..."

No sane person would have chosen for humanity to endure this stubbornly grinding pandemic. We must never allow ourselves to diminish, least of all to forget, the reality of the pain and losses this time of plague has brought. That said, if we look hard enough there are some silver linings in all that we are experiencing, and one of those is the advent of online ministries. An irony of this time of loss—which it has been and continues to be—is that the footprint of our parish is larger than ever. We now minister to more people than ever, and that number grows every week. Each week on our social media platforms we see new names, and a number of those whom we first met online are now finding their way to in-person participation. Surely no sane person would have chosen this pandemic, and yet we are wise to look for what we can take from it and build on moving forward. What has been given to us, and to all Christian ministries now online, is a whole new way to be the Church. There are no longer any inherent limits as to who can be part of a congregation because said congregation can now be *anywhere in the world* where people are connected to the internet. As ministers, we *all* have the challenge going forward of rebuilding the in-person component of congregational life while at the same time continuing to build the online component—and to do both with equal conviction. We have more work before us now than ever: more opportunities now than ever to share the Gospel. This is your ministry, and mine. Good *can* come from this otherwise painful and unsettling time.

In introducing his comments on Ephesians 4:1–16, N. T. Wright refers to its "majestic exhortation."[4] It is indeed one of the great passages in all of the Pauline literature. In his introductory comments on the passage Carl Holladay notes the shift from "doctrinal instruction [in chapters 1–3] to [in chapters 4–6] ethical exhortation."[5] There is that word again—*exhortation*. In chapter four Paul shifts from talk of doctrine to that of practical application—*praxis*—challenging us to translate doctrinal understanding into everyday Christian living. In concluding comments on our passage, Holladay states: "what is sought is a community of persons who are organically connected, whose common purpose is advanced, not hindered, by their diverse gifts, where growth and vitality are the norm, not the exception."[6] Amen.

---

1. *The Book of Common Prayer* (New York: The Seabury Press, 1979), 855.
2. *Ibid.*
3. Cally Hammond, "9th Sunday after Trinity." *Church Times.* 22 July 2021. https://www.churchtimes.co.uk/articles/2021/30-july/faith/sunday-s-readings/9th-sunday-after-trinity
4. N. T. Wright, *Twelve Months of Sundays: Biblical Meditations on the Christian Years A, B & C* (New York: Morehouse Publishing, 2012), 222.
5. Carl R. Holladay, "Acts 4:1–16." *Preaching Through the Christian Year (Year B): A Comprehensive Commentary on the Lectionary.* Fred B. Craddock, John H. Hayes, Carl R. Holladay, Gene M. Tucker, Contributors (Harrisburg, PA: Trinity Press International, 1993), 365.
6. *Ibid.*

23
IS IT LOVING?

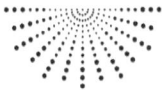

EPHESIANS 4:25–5:2 • 8 AUGUST 2021
ELEVENTH SUNDAY AFTER PENTECOST

²⁵So then, putting away falsehood, let all of us speak the truth to our neighbors, for we are members of one another. ²⁶Be angry but do not sin; do not let the sun go down on your anger, ²⁷and do not make room for the devil. ²⁸Thieves must give up stealing; rather let them labor and work honestly with their own hands, so as to have something to share with the needy. ²⁹Let no evil talk come out of your mouths, but only what is useful for building up, as there is need, so that your words may give grace to those who hear. ³⁰And do not grieve the Holy Spirit of God, with which you were marked with a seal for the day of redemption. ³¹Put away from you all bitterness and wrath and anger and wrangling and slander, together with all malice, ³²and be kind to one another, tenderhearted, forgiving one another, as God in Christ has forgiven you. ¹Therefore be imitators of God, as beloved children, ²and live in love, as Christ loved us and gave himself up for us, a fragrant offering and sacrifice to God.

When I graduated from seminary I was 27 years old. There would be nothing noteworthy about that now, but back then it was unusual for a seminarian in the Episcopal Church to be so young. In those days the Episcopal Church had bought into the notion that clergy needed to have "life experience," and thus the Church intentionally held off on identifying young ordinands. When I first felt the tug of the call to ordained ministry in the Episcopal Church it took some time for me to summon the courage to talk to a priest about it. And I do mean courage. I was painfully shy back then, and it was hard for me even to say the words: "I think I'm being called into the ministry." But the moment finally came and I said the words. The priest all but patted me on the head. His reply: "Come back when you're 40." My response: "That's 17 years from now!" His only response: "Well, we want our clergy to have life experience." The Episcopal Church has, for the most part, learned from its mistake regarding young ordinands. We lost an entire generation of priests and deacons to that mentality.

When I was ordained at 27, my bishop was brand new to the episcopate. Robert Hodges Johnson had just been ordained a bishop mere months before I was to be ordained a deacon. And so on the night of my ordination we had a young ordinand on the one hand, and a new bishop on the other, about to conduct a first for both. Just before the service there came a moment in the sacristy when it was just the two of us left in the room, and the bishop walked toward me right before the bell was to ring. All these years later I can still remember thinking in real time: This is going to be good. One last bit of profound pastoral wisdom before the service. Or, maybe we are about to pray together. Here is what actually happened. The bishop smiled and said: "Well kid, let's try to get this right."

Bob Johnson is a good man. He was always gracious in his support of his clergy. But what I really remember Bishop Johnson for, besides that moment before my ordination, is that he used to say both to the laity and to the clergy in the diocese: "Always remember, before you do or say anything, ask yourself the question: 'Is it loving?'" Now that really is pastoral wisdom. Before you do or say anything ask yourself the question: *Is it loving*?

Sometimes being loving requires confrontation. Sometimes it requires the willingness to discipline. But even then we are wise to ask ourselves: Is what I am doing the right thing? Is it the most loving action possible? In whatever situation we find ourselves, before we say or do anything we are indeed wise to ask ourselves: Is it loving? Is it the most Christ-like response given the circumstance? Another way to frame the question is: What would Christ have me do?

In Ephesians 4:29 we read: "Let no evil talk come out of your mouths, but only what is useful for building up..." How is that for pastoral wisdom? "Let no evil talk come out of your mouths, but only what is useful for building up, as there is need, so that your words may give grace to those who hear."

In the Greek of the New Testament the word translated here as "evil" can also be translated as "foul": "Let no foul talk come out of your mouths..." But the most literal translation of the Greek is "rotten." Both "foul" and "evil" are correct, but the most literal translation of the Greek is: "Let no rotten talk come out of your mouths, but only what is useful for building up, as there is need, so that your words may give grace to those who hear." I love the phrasing in the middle of this verse: "but only what is useful for building up..."

James 3:1–12 forms an entire section in the epistle on the importance of speech. In *The HarperCollins Study Bible* the section heading over James 3:1–12 reads: "Taming the tongue." In 3:5 we read: "the tongue is a small member, yet it boasts of great exploits." Classic biblical wisdom. The tongue is a *small* member, yet it boasts of *great* exploits. Which is a way of saying: With the tongue we can do great good. We can speak words of wisdom, words of encouragement, words of love, words of comfort. *And* with our tongue we can do great harm. We can speak words of hatred. Or we can show indifference. James cautions us to be careful as to how we use our speech. The same member can do good or evil.

Then in 3:9–10 we read: "With [the tongue] we bless the Lord and Father, and with it we curse those who are made in the likeness of God. From the same mouth come blessing and cursing. My brothers and sisters, this ought not to be so." More timeless biblical wisdom. With the tongue we can bless or curse. We can help or harm. We can build up or we can tear down. The choice is ours. From the same mouth can come blessing and cursing. So, I go back to Bishop Johnson. Before any words are spoken, or before any other action is taken, we are wise to remember, and that is the trick, to *remember* to ask ourselves the question: Is it loving? Will my response bring honor to Christ?

Back to Ephesians. In commenting on 4:29 N. T. Wright observes: "Your tongue gives you the opportunity to bring God's grace to people, by what you say and how you say it, and it's a shame to pass up this chance."[1] This is an important reminder. Over time most of us have countless opportunities to encourage people, to show Christ-like love and care. What a shame it is to pass up such opportunities.

C. Leslie Mitton writes of 4:29: "our conversation should aim at adding something good to the situation..."[2] While making a hospital call in the Emergency Room this past week, I literally could not help but overhear the situation in the next room over. The patient in that room was screaming, clearly in pain and having an understandably difficult time. But the patient was also out of control verbally. Given my years of experience in the ER, I knew full well that she was not looking for *my* help! But there was a person with her who clearly knew her at some level, whether she was a friend or a family member I do not know. There came a point in their conversation when her visitor said to the struggling patient: "What you're doing right now isn't helping." And she was right. Regardless of the patient's discomfort and frustration, her verbal abuse toward those trying to offer medical assistance was not helping. Yes, the patient was hurting. And yes, she was angry. And yet someone who loved her had the presence of mind to tell the truth: *What you're doing right now isn't helping.*

Our passage ends with 5:1–2: "Therefore be imitators of God, as beloved children, and live in love, as Christ loved us and give himself up for us, a fragrant offering and sacrifice to God." The word "live" here can also be translated "walk." *Walk in love...* Every choice we make matters, and in thinking about our choices we are wise to remember this timeless wisdom from the New Testament: *Be imitators of God, as beloved children*. But verse 1 starts with "Therefore..." To what does the "Therefore" refer? We have only to look back to 4:31–32. There what Paul is talking about is the fact that we have been forgiven by God. When *we* do wrong *we* are forgiven. And so "Therefore..." in 5:1 recalls our having been on the receiving end of Divine forgiveness. "Therefore be *imitators* (emphasis added) of God, as beloved children, and live (or walk) in love, as Christ loved us and gave himself up for us, a fragrant offering and sacrifice to God." The choices we make are meant to be made in response to God's grace. What we think. What we say. And what we do. "Therefore...walk in love..."

Peter S. Williamson notes regarding 5:1–2: "We cannot imitate God's omnipotence and omniscience, but we can imitate his forgiveness and generous love toward those who wrong us."[3] Our best intentions notwithstanding, we cannot reach our lofty spiritual ideals every single time, but the ideals are nonetheless clear. As we have been loved and forgiven by God in Christ, in response, we then are to *choose* grace.

Once more, timeless spiritual counsel from Ephesians 5:1–2: "Therefore be imitators of God, as beloved children, and live in love, as Christ loved us and gave himself up for us, a fragrant offering and sacrifice to God." In her commentary on 5:1–2, Cally Hammond writes: "it is a precious reminder of our high calling."[4] Amen.

---

1. N. T. Wright, *Paul for Everyone: The Prison Letters (Ephesians, Philippians, Colossians and Philemon)*. Second Edition (Louisville: Westminster John Knox Press, 2004), 56.
2. C. Leslie Mitton, *Ephesians*. The New Century Bible. Ronald E. Clements and Matthew Black, General Editors (Grand Rapids: William B. Eerdmans Publishing Company, 1973), 171.
3. Peter S. Williamson, *Ephesians*. Catholic Commentary on Sacred Scripture. Peter S. Williamson and Mary Healy, Series Editors (Grand Rapids: Baker Academic, 2009), 136.
4. Cally Hammond, "10th Sunday after Trinity." *Church Times*. 29 July 2021. https://www.churchtimes.co.uk/articles/2021/6-august/faith/sunday-s-readings/10th-sunday-after-trinity

24
WATCH HOW YOU WALK

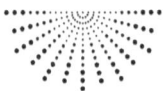

EPHESIANS 5:15–20 • 15 AUGUST 2021
TWELFTH SUNDAY AFTER PENTECOST

¹⁵Be careful then how you live, not as unwise people but as wise, ¹⁶making the most of the time, because the days are evil. ¹⁷So do not be foolish, but understand what the will of the Lord is. ¹⁸Do not get drunk with wine, for that is debauchery; but be filled with the Spirit, ¹⁹as you sing psalms and hymns and spiritual songs among yourselves, singing and making melody to the Lord in your hearts, ²⁰giving thanks to God the Father at all times and for everything in the name of our Lord Jesus Christ.

∼

I have a memory from childhood of being at family gatherings and hearing the adults say: "Time just flies by." It is a strong and lasting memory, hearing the grown-ups talking about how time seems to move faster and faster with age. At the time, I did not fully understand what they meant, but now I do. We all know the rhetorical question: "Where does the time go?" We may even find *ourselves* asking that question. More and more I find myself saying: "It seems like just yesterday..."

Lately I have been traveling back and forth frequently to my hometown in North Carolina. As I make that trip more often these days, I realize that it seems like just yesterday that I was 27 years old, and being ordained deacon in St. Mark's Episcopal Church, Gastonia, North Carolina. It seems like just yesterday..., but in reality it was 31 years ago. Memories of that night remain fresh in my mind. I well remember the combination of nervousness mixed with excitement. I can remember the support of my family and friends, and of future parishioners from St. Andrew's Episcopal Church, Canton, in the Diocese of Western North Carolina. It seems like only yesterday. But it was not. I can remember it all as if it were just yesterday. But it was not.

I had an interesting experience a couple of weeks ago in my home county. I was about to introduce myself to a therapist who was working with my mother in her rehabilitation. I wanted to thank the therapist for what she was doing on behalf of my mother, to let her know who I was and why I was in the room, and that I would be coming and going on a regular basis. So I walked over to her slowly, smiled and said "Hello," and tried to thank her for all that she was doing for my mother. But after telling her my name she interjected: "Oh, I know who you are. I've seen your father." A nice moment, except for the fact that my father is on the cusp of being 88 years old! Where *does* the time go?

When we think about it deeply enough, we may regard time as our most precious commodity. Whatever our gifts and talents, whatever our interests and passions, what can we do with them without time?

In Ephesians 5:15 Paul writes: "Be careful then how you live..." The Greek can be translated more literally: "Watch how you walk..." "Be careful then how you live—or, "Watch how you walk—not as unwise people but as wise, making the most of the time."

Practical life wisdom is of foundational importance in the Judeo-Christian tradition. Nearly every Sunday in this church we have a lesson from the Psalms. The Psalms are filled with practical, actionable spiritual wisdom. Earlier, we read in Psalm 34:13–14: "Keep your tongue from evil-speaking and your lips from lying words. Turn from evil and do good; seek peace and pursue it." Today's first lesson is a reading from Proverbs, the quintessential wisdom text in the Old Testament. The first line of Proverbs 9:1–6 begins: "*Wisdom* (emphasis added) has built her house..." The passage concludes: "Lay aside immaturity, and live, and walk in the way of insight." And then we come to our passage from Ephesians: "Be careful then how you live, not as unwise people but as wise..."

In his commentary on our passage, Peter S. Williamson writes: "'wisdom' is a concise way to describe the Christian way of life."[1] Week by week Christians the world over gather for worship, in part to help equip ourselves for continued life in the world, and what is more important to that equipping than the pursuit of wisdom? Williamson also notes: "Biblical wisdom is not theoretical or scientific knowledge but rather inspired practical understanding about how to live..."[2]

Andrew Lincoln comments on our passage: "To live as a wise person is not just to have knowledge but to have skill in living..."[3] Biblical wisdom is not concerned with the accumulation of knowledge in a vacuum. Instead, biblical wisdom equips us with practical tools for living a Christ-centered, Christ-focused life. Carl Holladay has written of our passage: "[Christians] are called to be deliberate, thoughtful, and self-reflective."[4]

"Be careful then how you live, not as unwise people but as wise, making the most of the time..." "Making the most of the time" can be translated: "redeeming the time..." While preparing this sermon I thought at one point about coupons. Yes, coupons! Most of you will access coupons with your cell phone, but I still clip them out of the newspaper. They come in handy, don't they? Why not save a little money when we can? But what good is a coupon if we do not use it? Of what value is a coupon if it is not redeemed? An unredeemed coupon is merely ink on a piece of paper, or just a digital image on your cell phone. A coupon that goes unredeemed is of no practical value.

The practical spiritual wisdom on offer in our passage is meant to help us redeem the time that we have and to make the most of it. To use it. And we are meant to be careful how we live. In other words: "Watch how you walk..." Time is precious. The Greek word for "time" in this verse is *kairos*, not *chronos*. *Chronos* refers to time as we normally experience it. *Kairos*, on the other hand, refers more to a nonlinear view of time. In 5:16 *kairos* can be translated "opportunity," and thus 5:15–16 can be rendered: "Be careful then how you live, not as unwise people but as wise, using the present opportunity to the fullest..."

Yet another way of translating "making the most of the time" is "making every moment count." The Greek here offers meaningfully nuanced ways of expressing the same basic concept. Paul is urging us to realize that we all have a finite amount of time in this life, and that to be a follower of Christ is to see the value of the opportunities we are given to know, and to share his love and grace.

I do not know about you, but I could have gone the rest of my life without hearing the term "Delta variant." Can I get an "Amen" in the Episcopal Church? Seriously, we could have gone the rest of our lives without the Delta variant. I really can remember as if it were yesterday getting into my car on May 13, turning on the radio for a news update, and hearing the announcement from the Centers for Disease Control that fully vaccinated people were free to remove their masks both indoors and outdoors. Remember that feeling of relief? Remember that joy? The excitement? At that point we had earned and could feel a renewed sense of hope. And yet... The caveat was always there: *But we are not out of the woods yet.* It was always there. Our best medical experts kept telling us: Yes, we are making progress. Yes, there is hope. But the pandemic is not over. The caveat has always been there. But we clearly have made progress. The director of the National Institutes of Health, Dr. Francis Collins, was on television again this past week. Though he does not wear it on his sleeve, Dr. Collins is a Christian and is not ashamed to say so. He noted this past week that we are not where we were a year ago, that we *are* making progress, and that there is reason to hope. But we still have to be vigilant. What Dr. Collins is calling us to is a practical wisdom. This is not a time for despair. It *is* a time for having the wisdom to follow the best medical advice and to make the best decisions we can, not just for ourselves, but for our neighbors. The choice before us transcends partisan politics. It is a moral and a spiritual choice—to be wise. *Watch how you walk...*

Please God, may those of us who live through this pandemic come away from it with a deepened appreciation for the gift of time, making every moment count going forward and seeing time for what it is: a precious and a fleeting gift. Our epistle lesson offers us timeless biblical wisdom. Ephesians 5:15–20 is just as relevant to us today, just as practical, just as actionable as it was to its original audience two millennia ago. These words apply to every single one of us especially now, given all that we have been through, and given the challenges still ahead of us: "Be careful then how you live, not as unwise people but as wise, making the most of the time..." Amen.

---

1. Peter S. Williamson, *Ephesians*. Catholic Commentary on Sacred Scripture. Peter S. Williamson and Mary Healy, Series Editors (Grand Rapids: Baker Academic, 2009), 149.
2. *Ibid.*
3. Andrew T. Lincoln, *Word Biblical Commentary: Ephesians*. Volume 12. Bruce M. Metzger, David A. Hubbard and Glenn W. Barker, General Editors (Nashville: Thomas Nelson Publishers, 1990), 341.
4. Carl R. Holladay, "Ephesians 5:15–20." *Preaching Through the Christian Year (Year B): A Comprehensive Commentary on the Lectionary*. Fred B. Craddock, John H. Hayes, Carl R. Holladay, Gene M. Tucker, Contributors (Harrisburg, PA: Trinity Press International, 1993), 379.

25
STAND FIRM

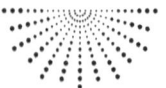

EPHESIANS 6:10–20 • 22 AUGUST 2021
THIRTEENTH SUNDAY AFTER PENTECOST

¹⁰Finally, be strong in the Lord and in the strength of his power. ¹¹Put on the whole armor of God, so that you may be able to stand against the wiles of the devil. ¹²For our struggle is not against enemies of blood and flesh, but against the rulers, against the authorities, against the cosmic powers of this present darkness, against the spiritual forces of evil in the heavenly places. ¹³Therefore take up the whole armor of God, so that you may be able to withstand on that evil day, and having done everything, to stand firm. ¹⁴Stand therefore, and fasten the belt of truth around your waist, and put on the breastplate of righteousness. ¹⁵As shoes for your feet put on whatever will make you ready to proclaim the gospel of peace. ¹⁶With all of these, take the shield of faith, with which you will be able to quench all the flaming arrows of the evil one. ¹⁷Take the helmet of salvation, and the sword of the Spirit, which is the word of God. ¹⁸Pray in the Spirit at all times in every prayer and supplication. To that end keep alert and always persevere in supplication for all the saints. ¹⁹Pray also for me, so that when I speak, a message may be given to me to make known with boldness the mystery of

the gospel, [20]for which I am an ambassador in chains. Pray that I may declare it boldly, as I must speak.

~

Debbie and I were invited to come to St. Luke's in 2003 and be part of this congregation's life, and we remain grateful for that invitation. For a year Debbie continued to work in Chattanooga, and then accepted a teaching position at Walker Valley High School as soon as the opportunity presented itself. Upon joining the faculty at Walker Valley here in Bradley County she found herself the only Episcopalian in a sea of Baptists and Pentecostals! Of course, I say "here in Bradley County" with love and affection. Debbie and I both grew up in staunch Baptist families, and in my youth I went with my family to many a Pentecostal singin' on Saturday nights. Suffice it to say, finding ourselves in a sea of Baptists and Pentecostals is not new to us.

Early in Debbie's time at Walker Valley the subject came up among her colleagues as to what the Episcopal Church says about the Second Coming of Christ. When asked the question directly, Debbie answered: "Not much." And she was right. We do not talk about it much. In some Christian traditions, so much emphasis is placed on the Second Coming that there is not enough emphasis placed on how we should live in the here and now. In the Episcopal Church we trust that the Lord *will* return, in the Lord's time. We affirm that belief Sunday after Sunday in reciting the Nicene Creed. But we also believe that *now* is the moment we have. *Now* are our opportunities to serve the Lord with gladness.

In just a few moments, in reciting the Creed we will say: "He will come again in glory to judge the living and the dead, and his kingdom will have no end."[1] We do believe in the Second Coming of Christ! We just do not talk about it nearly so much as is the case in some other traditions.

Along these lines, I well remember when one of our parishioners was being received into the Episcopal Church from Roman Catholicism. She may be watching online right now. During our final meeting before the bishop's visitation she said: "I just have one question: Do I get to keep the Virgin Mary?" Of course, I knew what she meant. And I said: "Yes! You may keep the Virgin Mary." Again, in just a few moments we will say: "by the power of the Holy Spirit he became incarnate from the Virgin Mary..."[2]

Every Church tradition has its points of emphasis. This is in part what makes the different denominations distinctive from each other. There are some Christians for whom "spiritual warfare" is a steady topic of conversation. Indeed, there are some traditions in which spiritual warfare is the *primary* conversation. While in college I was introduced to a bookseller called Christian Book Distributors. CBD is still going strong, and they distribute numerous catalogs throughout the year listing vast numbers of Christian books at discounted prices. It can safely be said that over the last forty years I have done my part to help keep Christian Book Distributors in business. On one particular day while placing an order I asked the customer service representative on the other end of the call: "Does something on your screen indicate what a loyal customer I am?" Her response was immediate: "Oh yes! I can see that." In most of CBD's catalogs there is an entire section dedicated to "Spiritual Warfare." And there are dozens of titles in that category.

The Episcopal Church does acknowledge the reality of spiritual warfare even though we do not use the term often. Do any of these questions sound familiar to you? "Do you renounce Satan and all the spiritual forces of wickedness that rebel against God?"[3] "Do you renounce the evil powers of this world which corrupt and destroy the creatures of God?"[4] "Do you renounce all sinful desires that draw you from the love of God?"[5] Sound familiar? These probing questions come from our baptismal liturgy. These are the questions we ask those about to be baptized. In our Prayer Book service of Holy Baptism we acknowledge the reality of spiritual warfare. Later on in the liturgy we ask not just the person(s) being baptized but the entire congregation: "Will you persevere in *resisting evil* (emphasis added), and, whenever you fall into sin, repent and return to the Lord?"[6] And we say in response: "I will, with God's help."[7]

Though in the Episcopal Church we may not talk a lot about spiritual warfare, we know that it is real. And yet week after week in our worship we claim that the love of God is stronger than the power of evil. Here I am reminded of that beautiful line in the Prologue to the Gospel of John: "The light shines in the darkness, and the darkness did not overcome it."[8] This verse acknowledges the reality of spiritual warfare and yet makes clear that the light of Christ shines in the darkness. The love of God *is* stronger than the power of evil.

Ephesians 6:10–20 is the climactic passage to which everything else in the epistle builds. In his commentary on the passage, Marcus Maxwell writes that it is: "one of the most well-known passages of the New Testament."[9] And in his commentary, Peter S. Williamson writes: "As in any good motivational speech, Paul's concluding exhortation is full of verbs in the imperative—it is a call to action."[10] Listen for the imperatives in verses 10–11: "Finally, be strong in the Lord and in the strength of his power. Put on the whole armor of God, so that you may be able to stand against the wiles of the devil." Here Paul is not talking about earthly governments; he is talking about the universal presence of evil. And then in verses 12–13: "For our struggle is not against enemies of blood and flesh, but against the rulers, against the authorities, against the cosmic powers of this present darkness, against the spiritual forces of evil in the heavenly places. Therefore take up the whole armor of God..." Our passage is a call to vigilance *and* action. It is an acknowledgement of the temptation we all face to violate our core principles. But in reminding us of that temptation, Paul is saying that the love of God, the love of Christ, is always stronger than the power of evil. In his commentary on our passage Darrell Bock writes these haunting words: "The struggle is pictured as hand-to-hand combat."[11] The struggle of good versus evil.

In my personal reading, one of my go-to subjects is C. S. Lewis. I seem to have an ever-growing number of benign obsessions, and one of them is C. S. Lewis. About every third or fourth book I read for 'fun' is a biography of Lewis. One of the better biographies is by Alan Jacobs of Wheaton College in Illinois. Jacobs has a passage in his book, *The Narnian: The Life and Imagination of C. S. Lewis*, in which he talks about Lewis' return to Christianity. Though having been baptized as an infant in an Anglican parish in Belfast, in his adolescence and young adulthood Lewis became a militant atheist. But in his late twenties, Lewis began to turn back to faith. He first came back to theism, a general belief in God, and then eventually reclaimed his Christianity. Lewis writes about his journey back to Christianity in his autobiography, *Surprised by Joy*, and Alan Jacobs says about Lewis' own description of his conversion: "C. S. Lewis never wrote anything more magnificent..." than that section of *Surprised by Joy* where Lewis himself talks about his conversion back to believing that Jesus Christ was Lord.[12] The language of Jacobs I really want us to take on board is: *C. S. Lewis never wrote anything more magnificent...* And it is my contention that Paul never wrote anything more magnificent than Ephesians 6:10–20.

Again, listen for the imperatives, the calls to action, in 6:10–17:

> Finally, be strong in the Lord and in the strength of his power. Put on the whole armor of God, so that you may be able to stand against the wiles of the devil. For our struggle is not against enemies of blood and flesh, but against the rulers, against the authorities, against the cosmic powers of this present darkness, against the spiritual forces of evil in the heavenly places. Therefore take up the whole armor of God, so that you may be able to withstand on that evil day, and having done everything, to stand firm. Stand therefore, and fasten the belt of truth

around your waist, and put on the breastplate of righteousness. As shoes for your feet put on whatever will make you ready to proclaim the gospel of peace. With all of these, take the shield of faith, with which you will be able to quench all the flaming arrows of the evil one. Take the helmet of salvation, and the sword of the Spirit, which is the word of God.

And then 6:18–20:

Pray in the Spirit at all times in every prayer and supplication. To that end keep alert and always persevere in supplication for all the saints. Pray also for me, so that when I speak, a message may be given to me to make known with boldness the mystery of the gospel, for which I am an ambassador in chains. Pray that I may declare it boldly, as I must speak.

It is magnificent, is it not? Beautiful, inspiring, aspirational and, in the end, reassuring. From one of the prison letters! Paul wrote this passage while imprisoned for his faith. These beautifully flowing—and compelling—words were not written in a spiritual vacuum. They were not written while Paul was on a restful and renewing spiritual retreat. From *prison*, knowing his likely fate, Paul wrote this magnificent passage, calling us to remember the ever-present love, grace—and strength—of Jesus Christ even in the midst of darkness.

It seems that every week now someone says to me: "I just cannot watch the news anymore." I hear it every week, and I want you to know that I *hear* what is being said. I have been a news junkie my whole life, always watching and listening to the news from as many different sources as possible—even as a school-age child. But these days, even I am not exposing myself quite as much as usual to the constant flow of bad news. "Moving history" or "history in motion," times such as ours are called. We are living in a time of moving history that will be remembered and studied for generations to come. But we are not studying it—we are in it!

We are experiencing history in motion as it unfolds. And there is a lot before us. There are so many challenges facing us as individuals and as a nation. So many challenges on so many fronts. My point is this: In the moment that is now we are not meant to read this magnificent passage from Ephesians in a spiritual vacuum. Paul's words first written for a specific time and place two millennia ago are available to us in our own time of great challenge, in this season of soul-searching for us all.

Our passage from Ephesians is, in the end, a call to action. *Look to Christ*, says Paul. Yes, there will always be temptation. Evil is ever-present. But Paul is assuring his readers then and now that, as Christians, we are equipped with both the knowledge and the spiritual gifts to meet times of challenge.

In all of this, it is crucially important for us to remember to have a sense of history. This is not the first time of soul-searching for our nation, and it will not be the last. There have always been periods of struggle in this country. There have always been challenges to be faced and acted upon, and we are in one of those moments now. To be sure, we are increasingly fatigued and disheartened in many ways. Yet there are also signs of great hope in this country even amidst our challenges.

I have a friend my age who remembers from his adolescence that every time he left the house his mother would say to him: "Remember who you are." Now that is some good parenting. Imagine, as a teenager, every time you left the house being instructed: *Remember who you are*. Week after week Christians the world over gather to remember who we are, and whose we are.

So, who—and whose—are we?

> Finally, be strong in the Lord and in the strength of his power. Put on the whole armor of God, so that you may be able to stand against the wiles of the devil. For our struggle is not against enemies of blood and flesh, but against the rulers, against the authorities, against the cosmic powers of this present darkness, against the spiritual forces of evil in the heavenly places.

Therefore take up the whole armor of God, so that you may be able to withstand on that evil day, and having done everything, to stand firm.

Amen.

---

1. *The Book of Common Prayer* (New York: The Seabury Press, 1979), 359.
2. *Ibid.*, 358.
3. *Ibid.*, 302.
4. *Ibid.*
5. *Ibid.*
6. *Ibid.*, 304.
7. *Ibid.*
8. John 1:5.
9. Marcus Maxwell, *Ephesians to Colossians and Philemon.* Daily Bible Commentary: A Guide for Reflection and Prayer (Peabody, MA: Hendrickson Publishers, 2007), 272.
10. Peter S. Williamson, *Ephesians.* Catholic Commentary on Sacred Scripture. Peter S. Williamson and Mary Healy, Series Editors (Grand Rapids: Baker Academic, 2009), 190.
11. Darrell L. Bock, *Ephesians.* Tyndale New Testament Commentaries. Volume 10. Eckhard J. Schnabel, Series Editor (Downers Grove, IL: InterVarsity Press, 2019), 196.
12. Alan Jacobs, *The Narnian: The Life and Imagination of C. S. Lewis* (New York: HarperOne, 2005), 129.

26
ACTION CONSONANT WITH CONVICTION

JAMES 1:17–27 • 29 AUGUST 2021
FOURTEENTH SUNDAY AFTER PENTECOST

[17] Every generous act of giving, with every perfect gift, is from above, coming down from the Father of lights, with whom there is no variation or shadow due to change. [18] In fulfillment of his own purpose he gave us birth by the word of truth, so that we would become a kind of first fruits of his creatures. [19] You must understand this, my beloved: let everyone be quick to listen, slow to speak, slow to anger; [20] for your anger does not produce God's righteousness. [21] Therefore rid yourselves of all sordidness and rank growth of wickedness, and welcome with meekness the implanted word that has the power to save your souls. [22] But be doers of the word, and not merely hearers who deceive themselves. [23] For if any are hearers of the word and not doers, they are like those who look at themselves in a mirror; [24] for they look at themselves and, on going away, immediately forget what they were like. [25] But those who look into the perfect law, the law of liberty, and persevere, being not hearers who forget but doers who act —they will be blessed in their doing. [26] If any think they are religious, and do not bridle their tongues but deceive their hearts, their religion is worthless. [27] Religion that is

pure and undefiled before God, the Father, is this: to care for orphans and widows in their distress, and to keep oneself unstained by the world.

From start to finish, the Epistle of James is packed full of accessible and practical spiritual wisdom in a way reminiscent of the books of Proverbs and Ecclesiastes. Every verse of James remains relevant to life in the twenty-first century. It really is an astonishing thing: a text nearly 2,000 years old that loses nothing over those two millennia. James is as useful to daily life in the twenty-first century as it was in the first century.

In some introductory comments on James, Luke Timothy Johnson writes: "The dominant mood of its verbs is the imperative."[1] And, "James exhorts his readers to action consonant with conviction."[2] Further, "James claims neither novelty nor depth. But no reader can mistake its lively voice or moral passion. Traditional teaching is given vibrancy in this exhortation to practical faith and active love."[3] In commenting on 1:17–27, Johnson notes: "For James, it is not the learning but the doing of wisdom that counts."[4]

The most famous critic of James was the reformer Martin Luther. Luther's view was that James concentrated too much on good works and therefore not enough on grace. Martin Luther famously said of the Epistle of James that it is "a right strawy epistle." But in reality, grace and works are two sides of the same coin. Divine grace inspires us to good works, and good works are the fruit of Divine grace. Works and grace are neither at odds with nor in competition with each other. They are, instead, two sides of the same coin.

In her introductory comments on our passage, Cally Hammond writes: "if I found myself in trouble, I would rather be met with the practical help of James than the noble theology of Romans."[5] Of course, James and Romans are not in competition with each other. Hammond's point is that, in a pinch, she would take the practical, everyday wisdom of James over the more sophisticated, philosophical theology found in the Epistle to the Romans.

Some of the most memorable verses in all of the Bible are found in the Epistle of James, including 1:19–21: "You must understand this, my beloved: let everyone be quick to listen, slow to speak, slow to anger; for your anger does not produce God's righteousness. Therefore rid yourselves of all sordidness and rank growth of wickedness, and welcome with meekness the implanted word that has the power to save your souls." Beautiful and flowing phrasing that is crystal clear in meaning. Let us please notice that James does not say: Do not get angry. That would be hopelessly unrealistic. It would be an impossible aspiration to try never to get angry. Anger is a natural human emotion. There are situations which *should* make us angry. There are times when we should *feel* anger. Even now we find ourselves in the midst of a season wherein there is much seething anger on numerous fronts. But James is clear: Be *slow* to anger. James does not want us to lose touch with our best selves by getting carried away and allowing anger to generate in us acts that we will come to regret—actions that we know are not in accord with God's will.

James does have a way with words. Let everyone be *quick* to listen, *slow* to speak, *slow* to anger. We find a related passage in Ephesians 4:26: "Be angry but do not sin; do not let the sun go down on your anger, and do not make room for the devil." Here the author is clear that anger is a natural emotion, an inevitable part of human existence. But as in James, so also in Ephesians we are cautioned not to let our anger get the better of us.

The book I am currently reading is Alan Jacobs' *The Narnian: The Life and Imagination of C. S. Lewis*. C. S. Lewis fought in World War I, arriving at the front in France on his nineteenth birthday. He suffered trench fever early in his time at the front, and then, three months into his tour, was wounded by 'friendly fire' and carried pieces of shrapnel in his body for the remainder of his life. Increasingly, scholars think that this shrapnel may well have contributed to the various health issues that shortened C. S. Lewis' life.

Having served in World War I, with the advent of World War II Lewis knew that it was incumbent upon him to encourage the people of Great Britain to show strength and perseverance amidst the difficult realities of war, and thus during the war years Lewis frequently left Oxford and traveled around the country speaking to various groups, including frequent trips to military bases to speak directly to the troops. You may know about Lewis' wartime broadcast talks on the BBC on Sunday nights. The contents of those broadcast talks would go on to constitute one of the classic books on Christian spirituality ever produced: *Mere Christianity*.

In the midst of World War II, Lewis wrote to his lifelong friend and correspondent Arthur Greeves: "It's a weary world, isn't it?"[6] Such haunting phrasing: *It's a weary world*.

It is a weary world in the moment that is now. We are wearied on multiple fronts. Here is just a little bit about my usual Sunday morning routine. Other than a brief conversation with Debbie, I spend early Sunday morning in complete silence. I get up at the exact same time every week, 5:40 a.m. I shave and shower at exactly the same time each Sunday. I eat the same breakfast at the same time every Sunday: a fried bologna and egg sandwich, with a side of fruit, at 6:45 a.m. And here is the point I am getting to. On a typical Sunday morning I do not turn on the radio, nor the television. I like complete silence on Sunday mornings before I get to church so that I can focus on and get prepared for my responsibilities for the day. But *this* Sunday morning, as I drove in I had to turn on the radio to see if anything else(!) had happened overnight that might impact my words today. It really is a wearying time for the world, and we are a weary nation in a way not seen since the late 1960s and on into the early 1970s.

It is my privilege week after week to stand in this pulpit and offer spiritual reflections and encouragement drawn from the riches of Holy Scripture and the Christian tradition. It is my calling, my vocation, to offer us all spiritual encouragement each week. You will notice that I say *us* and not *you*. Some of the best preaching advice I have ever heard is: Preach *to* yourself, not *of* yourself. I try to follow that advice, and thus my sermons are for *me* every bit as much as they are for you, and I have needed spiritual encouragement during this last year and a half just as you have. And on this particular Sunday morning I need spiritual encouragement every bit as much as you do. We gather on Sundays to celebrate and nurture our unity in Christ. We are sisters and brothers in Christ—family—and we can take encouragement in that. Christians gather, in part, to acknowledge and celebrate our unity in Christ. And in the Church we are meant to celebrate our essential *unity in Christ* even amidst our diversity of thought and experiences. Especially in the midst of this wearying season in which we find ourselves, we gather in worship for encouragement, and for spiritual guidance and strength to meet the challenges before us. That being said, the words of the liturgy, the music, and the sermon must be connected to reality—life's oftentimes harsh realities. Some of the other best preaching advice I have ever heard comes from the biblical theologian Karl Barth, who held that in preparing a sermon the preacher should have the Bible in one hand and a newspaper in the other. Of course, Barth's point is that sound Christian preaching must be both solidly grounded in Scripture *and* meaningfully connected to our present-day realities.

It is a weary world, and we are a weary nation. So many of us are understandably frustrated, even angry, on several fronts. But in the end we must face the question: How do we deal with all of this? How do we respond to such a challenging time? And, how do we, as followers of Jesus Christ, maintain our faith and offer a message of hope to the wider culture? With all of this in mind, I cannot imagine a better passage for the lectionary to have given us today than James 1:17–27, which includes: "let everyone be quick to listen, slow to speak, slow to anger; for your anger does not produce God's righteousness." James is encouraging us: Remember who you are. And: Remember *whose* you are. *There-*

fore rid yourselves of all sordidness and rank growth of wickedness, and welcome with meekness [or humility] *the implanted word that has the power to save your souls.* Even in the midst of a grinding, wearying global pandemic, as people of faith we gather weekly either in person or online to receive again the *implanted word*, the ancient and inspired wisdom of Scripture. Especially in this time of nationwide, indeed global, weariness, anxiety, and anger, it is crucial for us to remember that our response is meant to be firmly grounded in the words and work of Jesus Christ.

The Epistle of James includes some of the most memorable passages in all of the Bible, including 1:27: "Religion that is pure and undefiled before God, the Father, is this: to care for orphans and widows in their distress..." "Orphans and widows" in the ancient world was code for *all people in need*. The ancient world did not offer the social safety nets that many (though certainly not all) of us take for granted, and thus to care for "orphans and widows" means to care for *all* who are in particular need and have none to help them. *Religion that is pure and undefiled before God, the Father, is this: to care for orphans and widows in their distress, and to keep oneself unstained by the world.*

It is a weary world, and we are a weary nation. But this is no time for people of faith to shrink back. This is, instead, a time for people of faith to step forward.

This past Thursday, thirteen brave Americans were killed in a terrorist attack in Kabul as they were caring heroically and selflessly for 'orphans and widows' in their distress. They are:

Marine Corps Lance Cpl. Rylee J. McCollum, 20,
Jackson, Wyoming

Marine Corps Lance Cpl. Jared M. Schmitz, 20,
Wentzville, Missouri

Marine Corps Lance Cpl. David Lee Espinoza, 20,
Rio Bravo, Texas

Navy Hospital Corpsman Maxton W. Soviak, 22,
Berlin Heights, Ohio

Marine Corps Lance Cpl. Hunter Lopez, 22,
Indio, California

Marine Corps Lance Cpl. Kareem Mae'Lee Grant Nikoui, 20,
Norco, California

Marine Corps Staff Sgt. Darin Taylor Hoover, 31,
Midvale, Utah

Marine Corps Cpl. Daegan William-Tyeler Page, 23,
Omaha, Nebraska

Army Staff Sgt. Ryan Knauss, 23,
Corryton, Tennessee

Marine Corps Sgt. Johanny Rosario Pichardo, 25,
Lawrence, Massachusetts

Marine Corps Cpl. Humberto A. Sanchez, 22,
Logansport, Indiana

Marine Corps Sgt. Nicole Leeann Gee, 23,
Roseville, California

Marine Corps Lance Cpl. Dylan Ryan Merola, 20,
Rancho Cucamonga, California

These American heroes died in action consonant with their conviction. Amen.

1. Luke Timothy Johnson, "James." *Harper's Bible Commentary.* James L. Mays, General Editor (San Francisco: Harper & Row, Publishers, 1988), 1272.
2. *Ibid.*
3. *Ibid.*
4. *Ibid.*, 1273.
5. Cally Hammond, "13th Sunday after Trinity." *Church Times.* 19 August 2021. https://www.churchtimes.co.uk/articles/2021/27-august/faith/sunday-s-readings/13th-sunday-after-trinity
6. Alan Jacobs, *The Narnian: The Life and Imagination of C. S. Lewis* (New York: HarperOne, 2005), 225.

27

THE SIN OF DISCRIMINATION

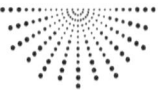

JAMES 2:1–10, 14–17 • 05 SEPTEMBER 2021
FIFTEENTH SUNDAY AFTER PENTECOST

¹My brothers and sisters, do you with your acts of favoritism really believe in our glorious Lord Jesus Christ? ²For if a person with gold rings and in fine clothes comes into your assembly, and if a poor person in dirty clothes also comes in, ³and if you take notice of the one wearing the fine clothes and say, "Have a seat here, please," while to the one who is poor you say, "Stand there," or, "Sit at my feet," ⁴have you not made distinctions among yourselves, and become judges with evil thoughts? ⁵Listen, my beloved brothers and sisters. Has not God chosen the poor in the world to be rich in faith and to be heirs of the kingdom that he has promised to those who love him? ⁶But you have dishonored the poor. Is it not the rich who oppress you? Is it not they who drag you into court? ⁷Is it not they who blaspheme the excellent name that was invoked over you? ⁸You do well if you really fulfill the royal law according to the scripture, "You shall love your neighbor as yourself." ⁹But if you show partiality, you commit sin and are convicted by the law as transgressors. ¹⁰For whoever keeps the whole law but fails in one point has become accountable for all of it. ¹⁴What good is it, my brothers and sisters,

if you say you have faith but do not have works? Can faith save you? ¹⁵If a brother or sister is naked and lacks daily food, ¹⁶and one of you says to them, "Go in peace; keep warm and eat your fill," and yet you do not supply their bodily needs, what is the good of that? ¹⁷So faith by itself, if it has no works, is dead.

∼

The Epistle of James offers some of the most memorable verses in all of the Bible. We may think of James 1:22: "But be doers of the word, and not merely hearers..." Or 1:27: "Religion that is pure and undefiled before God, the Father, is this: to care for orphans and widows in their distress, and to keep oneself unstained by the world." And then there is 2:17: "So faith by itself, if it has no works, is dead."

Luke Timothy Johnson says of 2:1–10, 14–17: "James' reputation for vividness owes not a little to this passage."[1] Johnson is right. The words leap off the page and go a long way in helping to forge our moral consciousness.

In his commentary on our passage Kent Hughes writes: "James is preeminently a moral theologian."[2] The entire letter has to do with equipping us to be able to discern the difference between right and wrong. The Epistle of James is a wisdom text in the tradition of the Book of Proverbs in the Old Testament and the Book of Sirach found in the Apocrypha. Proverbs and Sirach are quintessential Jewish wisdom texts, and James carries the wisdom tradition into the New Testament era. From start to finish the Epistle of James offers practical, actionable spiritual wisdom. Its aim is to foster right behavior. Without question, James is first and foremost a moral theologian.

Our passage begins: "My brothers and sisters, do you with your acts of favoritism really believe in our glorious Lord Jesus Christ?" A probing question. The word for "favoritism" in the Greek text is unique to the New Testament; it does not occur in any other Greek literature of the period. About this Greek word translated "favoritism" James Adamson notes that it is among the earliest definitely Christian words.[3] The word appears to have been coined to address squarely the aspiration that within Christian congregations there is meant to be an atypical (for the time period) equality of membership regardless of socio-economic status. The Greek word literally means: to receive someone according to their face. "Favoritism" is to prejudge someone simply based on their appearance. Of course, what is meant to matter in congregational life is not a person's outward appearance, but his or her value in the eyes of God.

James' clear teaching is that we are to be ever wary of any type of favoritism in the life of the church. The New English Bible translates the verse: "My brothers and sisters, believing as you do in our Lord Jesus Christ who reigns in glory, you must never show snobbery..." So, in addition to favoritism, the word can be translated as snobbery. The New Jerusalem Bible has it: "My brothers, do not let class distinction enter into your faith in Jesus Christ." Whatever the nuanced differences in translation, James' teaching is unambiguous. Beware of snobbery in a Christian fellowship. Beware of class distinction. Do not judge someone solely on outward appearances.

One of the fine scholars on the Epistle of James is Sophie Laws. I have had Sophie Laws' commentary on James since 1990, the year of my ordination. In Laws' treatment of our passage the section heading reads: "The Sin of Discrimination."[4] How is that for clear, direct teaching? The *sin* of discrimination.

In our passage James uses his considerable storytelling ability to paint an obvious picture of favoritism. Our translation has it that a person with "gold rings" shows up for church. The more literal translation of the Greek is "gold fingers." What the Greek text is picturing is a person with a gold ring on every finger showing up for church. And then a poor person is referenced. In biblical Greek there are two words for poor. One simply refers to a person who does not own property. The other Greek word for poor means destitute. Two different words to depict varying levels of poverty. James uses the word for destitute.

It is worth noting that the more literal translation for "dirty" clothes in 2:2 is "filthy." James has skillfully crafted a scenario of obvious favoritism, and then he says in verse 8: "You do well if you really fulfill the royal law..." The term "royal law" is unique to James in the New Testament. "You do well if you really fulfill the royal law according to the scripture, 'You shall love your neighbor as yourself.'" Regardless of one's outward appearance, it is one's value in the eyes of God that defines who we are. The "royal law" for James is traced back to the teaching of Jesus, who traced his understanding back to Leviticus 19:18: "you shall love your neighbor as yourself..."

Again, 2:1: "My brothers and sisters, do you with your acts of favoritism *really* (emphasis added) believe in our glorious Lord Jesus Christ?" And then in verse 8: "You do well if you *really* (emphasis added) fulfill the royal law according to the scripture, 'You shall love your neighbor as yourself.'"

Sophie Laws hits it just right in her classic commentary on the Epistle of James. Our passage is squarely about the *sin* of discrimination. Whether we translate the Greek as favoritism, or snobbery, or class distinction, what James is saying is, in the end, crystal clear. It was clear to his original audience and it is clear to us: Beware of both overt and subtle prejudice. Beware of judging a child of God solely on their outward appearance.

In his commentary on our passage James Adamson notes: "This passage exemplifies the enduring value of the Epistle of James as a caution to us against any complacent illusion of progress."[5] We have to be intentional about keeping our actions in accord with our expressed theological beliefs. James *is* primarily a moral theologian. From start to finish, James offers pastoral wisdom that reminds us of the crucial importance of practicing what we preach.

Every small town typically has at least one legendary educator. One of my hometown's legendary teachers was "Miss Amy"

Smith. All these years later, memories of Miss Amy remain fresh in my mind. Amy Smith had taught my parents, and she was still teaching when my sister and I came along. One of my strongest memories of Miss Amy is that when one of us would have a breakthrough, she would be so pleased that she would extend her index finger and exclaim: "Raise the flag!" But when we were struggling, Miss Amy would encourage us with: "Don't be a Doubting Thomas."

I do not know who taught it to you, but it was Miss Amy Smith who taught me: "Don't judge a book by its cover." Fifty years on, and I can still remember the sound of her voice. Talk about practical, actionable wisdom for all times and circumstances. *Don't judge a book by its cover.* James said it differently, yet equally clearly, in his day and time: Beware of receiving someone according to their face. Amen.

---

1. Luke Timothy Johnson, *The Letter of James: A New Translation with Introduction and Commentary*. The Anchor Bible, Volume 37A. William Foxwell Albright and David Noel Freedman, General Editors (New York: Doubleday, 1995), 226.
2. R. Kent Hughes, *James: Faith that Works. Preaching the Word* (Wheaton, IL: Crossway Books, 1991), 98.
3. James B. Adamson, *The Epistle of James*. The New International Commentary on the New Testament. F. F. Bruce, Editor (Grand Rapids: William B. Eerdmans Publishing Company, 1976), 104.
4. Sophie Laws, *The Epistle of James*. Harper's New Testament Commentaries. Henry Chadwick, General Editor (San Francisco: Harper and Row, Publishers, 1980), 93.
5. Adamson, 107.

28
TAMING THE TONGUE

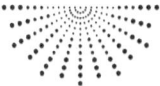

JAMES 3:1–12 • 12 SEPTEMBER 2021
SIXTEENTH SUNDAY AFTER PENTECOST

¹Not many of you should become teachers, my brothers and sisters, for you know that we who teach will be judged with greater strictness. ²For all of us make many mistakes. Anyone who makes no mistakes in speaking is perfect, able to keep the whole body in check with a bridle. ³If we put bits into the mouths of horses to make them obey us, we guide their whole bodies. ⁴Or look at ships: though they are so large that it takes strong winds to drive them, yet they are guided by a very small rudder wherever the will of the pilot directs. ⁵So also the tongue is a small member, yet it boasts of great exploits. How great a forest is set ablaze by a small fire! ⁶And the tongue is a fire. The tongue is placed among our members as a world of iniquity; it stains the whole body, sets on fire the cycle of nature, and is itself set on fire by hell. ⁷For every species of beast and bird, of reptile and sea creature, can be tamed and has been tamed by the human species, ⁸but no one can tame the tongue—a restless evil, full of deadly poison. ⁹With it we bless the Lord and Father, and with it we curse those who are made in the likeness of God. ¹⁰ From the same mouth come blessing and cursing. My brothers and sisters, this ought

not to be so. ⁱⁱDoes a spring pour forth from the same opening both fresh and brackish water? ¹²Can a fig tree, my brothers and sisters, yield olives, or a grapevine figs? No more can salt water yield fresh.

~

Dean Smith, one of the all-time great college basketball coaches, used to say: "I say what's on my mind. I just don't say everything that's on my mind." Timeless, practical wisdom. I say what's on my mind. I just don't say *everything* that's on my mind. The bishop who ordained me, Robert Johnson, used to remind us in the Diocese of Western North Carolina: "Before we do or say anything, we should always ask ourselves the question: Is it loving?" More timeless and practical wisdom. Before we do or say anything, we should ask ourselves the question: *Is it loving*? Is it kind? Will it build up? Or, will it tear down? Does it encourage? Or, will it hurt? Before we do or say anything, we should ask ourselves the question: Is it loving? We might sharpen that question even a bit more by asking ourselves: Is it Christ-like?

In commenting on James 3:1–12, Kent Hughes writes: "this is the most penetrating (and convicting) exposition of the tongue anywhere in literature, sacred or secular."[1] A strong statement. Our passage is indeed as cautionary a treatment on careful speech as exists. Luke Timothy Johnson notes: "James makes failure to control speech the very antithesis of authentic religion."[2] Another strong observation. James makes failure to control speech the very *antithesis* of *authentic* religion. To be sure, throughout Scripture we find teaching on careful speech. The psalmist writes in 141:3: "Set a guard over my mouth, O LORD; keep watch over the door of my lips." And Jesus himself says in Matthew 12:36: "I tell you, on the day of judgment you will have to give an account for every careless word you utter..."

In 3:2a James writes: "For all of us make many mistakes." *All* of us. In context, James is talking about teachers. But of course his words apply to us all, for indeed, we all make many mistakes. Some of the best preaching advice I have ever heard is: Preach to yourself, not of yourself. Possibly the *best* preaching advice I have ever head: Preach *to* yourself, not *of* yourself. Periodically someone will say to me on the way out of church: "God must have given you that message just for me." And I am glad to hear it. At other times I might hear: "Your sermon was just what I needed today." And, again, I am glad to hear it. But please let me say clearly: If you needed to hear it, then I needed to hear it too. Of course, I am grateful to hear encouragement and affirmation when a sermon has hit the mark. But I can assure you, if you needed to hear it, then I needed to hear it as well.

We are all on the journey of faith together. James makes that crystal clear. We all make many mistakes. James is careful to include himself. He is one of us. He is on our side.

The Epistle of James is, in reality, an epistle in literary form only. The text is, in fact, an early Christian sermon heavy on pastoral wisdom, and James is gracious in modeling a healthy sense of humility. We *all* make many mistakes. We are all meant to be diligent in taming the tongue. James is careful to preach *to* himself, not *of* himself.

In 3:5a we read: "the tongue is a small member, yet it boasts of great exploits." James then employs the remarkably vivid imagery of both a bridle bit in a horse's mouth and the rudder of a ship: both small, yet powerful instruments. Carl Holladay observes regarding 3:5: "small things can do great harm. Size is not the main measure of power."[3] That ill-chosen word we unthinkingly throw into a conversation. That careless, offhanded remark. That ill-considered joke. All might be uttered in an instant, and yet can do lasting harm if we have not taken care to think through what we say, if we have not asked ourselves: Is it loving? Is it kind? Will it help? Is it Christ-like? By the New Testament era, it had already been observed that we have two ears and one mouth for a reason. In his own inimitable way, James affirms such wisdom.

In 3:9–10 we read: "With [the tongue] we bless the Lord and

Father, and with it we curse those who are made in the likeness of God. From the same mouth come blessing and cursing. My brothers and sisters, this ought not to be so." Here we encounter some of the most profound teaching in all of literature on the importance of careful speech. James cautions followers of Christ: One minute we can be praising God with our speech, and the next minute we may cause offense to our sister or brother who is made in God's image. This simply ought not to be so.

The Greek here is forceful. The New Jerusalem Bible translates 3:10, "the blessing and curse come out of the same mouth. My brothers, this must be wrong." And The Common English Bible has it: "Blessing and cursing come from the same mouth. My brothers and sisters, it just shouldn't be this way!" A dynamic and haunting translation of the Greek: *it just shouldn't be this way*. How can we bless God in one breath, and then curse a child of God in the next?

The Epistle of James brings into the Christian era the tradition of Jewish wisdom, exemplified by the book of Proverbs in the Old Testament, and the book of Sirach in the Apocrypha. James is the great wisdom text of the New Testament—2,000 years old, and yet as fresh and as relevant today as it was to its original audience. Every word in the Epistle of James is of practical relevance to daily living in the twenty-first century. James has lost nothing in translation.

We are living in a particularly tense time in our culture, a time of deep, seemingly intractable divisions. There is a growing fatigue from the pandemic. We all feel it. And there is rising anger. We are all increasingly on edge. And thus, in the moment that is ours, in a sense words are more important to us than ever. The stakes regarding our use of the gift of speech are as high as at any other point in our lifetimes. In James' day, two millennia ago, the two primary platforms for speech were personal conversation and literature. They were the only two outlets for the exchange of words. Now we have television, radio, the telephone. Does anybody remember the telephone? There is text messaging, and ever-increasing numbers of social media platforms. We have more avenues for communication than ever. As a result, words come 'easier' than ever. We have more platforms, more opportunities for speech than at any other point in human history, and, consequently, it is more important than ever for us to think before we have our say, before we 'put it out there' in whatever form.

Is it loving? Or, even more precisely: Is it Christ-like? Amen.

---

1. R. Kent Hughes, *James: Faith that Works*. Preaching the Word (Wheaton, IL: Crossway Books, 1991), 143.
2. Luke Timothy Johnson, *The Letter of James: A New Translation with Introduction and Commentary*. The Anchor Bible, Volume 37A. William Foxwell Albright and David Noel Freedman, General Editors (New York: Doubleday, 1995), 264.
3. Carl R. Holladay, "Ephesians 5:15-20." *Preaching Through the Christian Year (Year B): A Comprehensive Commentary on the Lectionary*. Fred B. Craddock, John H. Hayes, Carl R. Holladay, Gene M. Tucker, Contributors (Harrisburg, PA: Trinity Press International, 1993), 410.

29
WISDOM FROM ABOVE

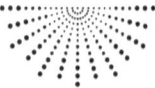

JAMES 3:13–4:3,7-8A • 19 SEPTEMBER 2021
SEVENTEENTH SUNDAY AFTER PENTECOST

¹³Who is wise and understanding among you? Show by your good life that your works are done with gentleness born of wisdom. ¹⁴But if you have bitter envy and selfish ambition in your hearts, do not be boastful and false to the truth. ¹⁵Such wisdom does not come down from above, but is earthly, unspiritual, devilish. ¹⁶For where there is envy and selfish ambition, there will also be disorder and wickedness of every kind. ¹⁷But the wisdom from above is first pure, then peaceable, gentle, willing to yield, full of mercy and good fruits, without a trace of partiality or hypocrisy. ¹⁸And a harvest of righteousness is sown in peace for those who make peace. ¹Those conflicts and disputes among you, where do they come from? Do they not come from your cravings that are at war within you? ²You want something and do not have it; so you commit murder. And you covet something and cannot obtain it; so you engage in disputes and conflicts. You do not have, because you do not ask. ³You ask and do not receive, because you ask wrongly, in order to spend what you get on your pleasures. ⁷Submit yourselves therefore to God.

Resist the devil, and he will flee from you. ⁸Draw near to God, and he will draw near to you.

~

In James 3:13a we read: "Who is wise and understanding among you?" In the Epistle of James, this is not merely a rhetorical question; it is *the* question. The Epistle of James is a wisdom text, standing in the tradition of wisdom texts such as Proverbs and Ecclesiastes in the Old Testament and the Book of Sirach in the Apocrypha. From start to finish, the Epistle of James is about the acquisition and application of spiritual wisdom. It is not merely one rhetorical question among many: "Who is wise and understanding among you?" For James, it is *the* question.

The first parish I served as an ordained minister was St. Andrew's Episcopal Church in Canton, North Carolina. Early on in my tenure there I learned of a man named Clyde Kelly, whom people simply referred to as Kelly. Kelly, I was told, came into town every day to have breakfast. He would bring with him his books and his papers, and would spend the morning drinking coffee, talking to people, and reading his books and writing in his journals. I was also told that he was the smartest man in the county, and that he was "a retired Harvard professor." All of which sparked my curiosity: How does a retired Harvard professor end up in Haywood County, North Carolina? As you can imagine, I wanted to meet this wisest man in the county. And eventually, I did. In due course, Kelly found St. Andrew's and became a member of the church, and he and I ended up having a deep, mutually beneficial pastoral relationship and personal friendship. But in my early days in Haywood County I just knew him as Kelly—the wise, eccentric, retired 'Harvard professor' who came into town every morning to have breakfast. Well, it turned out that Kelly was a retired electrician! I once asked him: "Have you ever even been to Harvard?" "Oh no. I've never even seen the place." A retired electrician, but still the wisest person anybody knew in Haywood County.

John Adams was one of the Founders of our country and served as our second president. John Adams had a lot to do with the system of checks and balances that serves as the foundation for our Constitution. He was a brilliant man. And his wife Abigail was a brilliant woman. John Adams was blessed with a long life; he lived many years after his tenure as president and stayed active the entire time. In his maturity, John Adams would reflect on his early career as a lawyer in Boston, and in reflecting on those days in colonial America, he remembered a certain shoemaker. Adams remembered this shoemaker being at peace with himself, and at peace with the people around him. This shoemaker was a good man who loved his work, loved his family, and loved his customers. In his maturity, John Adams remembered regarding this shoemaker: "I had scarcely got out the door before he began to sing again like a nightingale..."[1] The man was happy. He was at peace. And thus, in his retirement—in his maturity—John Adams asked the question, "Which was the greatest philosopher? Epictetus or this shoemaker?"[2] In the end, he was posing the question: Who is the wisest? The person with the most knowledge, or the person who knows the peace of mind of being comfortable in his or her own skin? Of course, the two are not mutually exclusive. And to be sure, one can inform the other. Who was the wisest? The great Epictetus, or a shoemaker in colonial Boston who knew peace of mind, happiness and joy?

We have to be clear when thinking about wisdom that wisdom and knowledge are not necessarily synonyms. One can be aware of all kinds of factual information and not be able to translate that knowledge into practical action. In asking the question, Adams is pressing us to think about wisdom vis-à-vis mere factual knowledge. James advocates for a practical, actionable, everyday spiritual wisdom. In 3:13b we read: "Show by your good life that your works are done with gentleness born of wisdom." This is practical, actionable spiritual counsel. For James, it is in our actions that we show true wisdom.

In commenting on our passage, Solomon Andria writes in *Africa Bible Commentary*: "Wisdom is not a philosophical theory but something that has to be demonstrated in daily life."[3] And Peter H. Davids notes in his commentary: "James states that not one's orthodoxy (right preaching) but one's orthopraxis (right living) is the mark of true wisdom."[4] True wisdom is practical. And it is daily. In the routine of life, true spiritual wisdom brings us a baseline peace of mind, and an ease with ourselves in our own skin.

And then in 3:17 we get: "But the wisdom from above is first pure, then peaceable, gentle, willing to yield, full of mercy and good fruits, without a trace of partiality, or hypocrisy." In 3:17 James offers a summation of everything else he has written up to this point in the epistle. Everything from 1:1 to 3:17 has been building to the question: What is true wisdom? In the middle of the epistle, in 3:17, we find our answer: *But the wisdom from above is first pure, then peaceable, gentle, willing to yield, full of mercy and good fruits, without a trace of partiality or hypocrisy.*

Let us ponder for a moment the phrase "willing to yield." Debbie is from the Gulf Coast of Florida, Pensacola to be exact, and most of her family is still there. Every time a storm approaches the panhandle of Florida, I watch the Weather Channel and follow the path of the storm. I want to know as much as possible about how people whom we love are about to be impacted. I am a weather nerd, by the way. You might not think that about me, but I am one of those people who can watch the Weather Channel for hours on end and be perfectly happy.

When a storm is threatening the panhandle, I am particularly attentive. And in watching the coverage of an approaching storm I always look for the palm trees in the background of the camera shot. In the midst of the storm, one can see the palm trees bending, maybe losing a branch here and there. They bend, they sway with the wind, but, more often than not, they do not break. They are flexible. They are 'willing to yield,' but they seldom break. This is what James is talking about in our passage. A willingness to yield is not a sign of weakness. To be willing to yield is to be flexible as we experience the realities of life. It is to be open-minded to different people and different points of view. Ultimately, *willing to yield* means accepting the given realities of life—the things we cannot change. We never have to agree with every point of view. But to be open-minded, to be willing to listen—to be willing to change over time—is what James is advocating. A part of practical spiritual wisdom is to be willing to yield, to be flexible. As we move forward in life, we grow wiser by taking in and reflecting upon new ideas and experiences, not by shutting them out. And we should be clear in reflecting on spiritual wisdom that advancing in age in and of itself does not guarantee advancing in wisdom. We have to be intentional about being open-minded, willing to yield, willing to evolve and grow over time. In his commentary on our passage, Kent Hughes writes: "A man or a woman is in a bad way when he or she is no longer persuadable."[5] Of course, we need not be persuaded by every idea or every action. But a general openness to different points of view and different life experiences—an intentional openness to what life continues to teach us—is a part of the practical wisdom that James espouses.

Many of you will know the poetry, the philosophy, of Rumi. Rumi was born in 1207 in modern-day Afghanistan. Born in *1207*, Rumi's works are still read today. He is as relevant today as he has ever been and is particularly popular in the United States. In his maturity, Rumi is remembered as having reflected: "Yesterday I was clever and wanted to change the world. Today I am wise and want to change myself." The self-reflective among us can see that progression in ourselves. We recognize that the more we learn, the less we 'know.' It is an observation for the ages: *Yesterday I was clever and wanted to change the world. Today I am wise and want to change myself.*

Of course, being open to ideas for change is a part of life.

Every generation needs its prophets who push for positive change. We need people fiercely advocating for change that will benefit those on the margins of society. Thank God for prophets. But a part of maturity, a part of an accumulating spiritual and practical wisdom is to realize increasingly over time: *I* do not have all the answers. And *we* as a culture do not have all the answers. Indeed, far from it. The wisdom for which James advocates is not simply the accumulation of more and more factual knowledge. Spiritual wisdom manifests in everyday life, in our fundamental attitudes and in our concrete actions.

Again, James 3:17: "But the wisdom from above is first pure, then peaceable, gentle, willing to yield, full of mercy and good fruits, without a trace of partiality or hypocrisy." Or, put another way: They will know we are Christians by our love. Amen.

---

1. David McCullough, *John Adams* (New York: Simon and Schuster Paperbacks, 2001), 570.
2. *Ibid.*, 571.
3. Solomon Andria, *Africa Bible Commentary*. Tokunboh Adeyemo, General Editor (Grand Rapids: Zondervan, 2006), 1539.
4. Peter H. Davids, *James*. New International Biblical Commentary. W. Ward Gasque, New Testament Editor (Peabody, MA: Hendrickson Publishers, Inc., 1989), 88.
5. R. Kent Hughes, *James: Faith that Works*. Preaching the Word (Wheaton, IL: Crossway Books, 1991), 159.

30
WELCOME TO THE CHURCH OF THE FUTURE

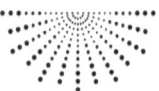

JAMES 5:13–20 • 25 SEPTEMBER 2021
EIGHTEENTH SUNDAY AFTER PENTECOST

[13] Are any among you suffering? They should pray. Are any cheerful? They should sing songs of praise. [14] Are any among you sick? They should call for the elders of the church and have them pray over them, anointing them with oil in the name of the Lord. [15] The prayer of faith will save the sick, and the Lord will raise them up; and anyone who has committed sins will be forgiven. [16] Therefore confess your sins to one another, and pray for one another, so that you may be healed. The prayer of the righteous is powerful and effective. [17] Elijah was a human being like us, and he prayed fervently that it might not rain, and for three years and six months it did not rain on the earth. [18] Then he prayed again, and the heaven gave rain and the earth yielded its harvest. [19] My brothers and sisters, if anyone among you wanders from the truth and is brought back by another, [20] you should know that whoever brings back a sinner from wandering will save the sinner's soul from death and will cover a multitude of sins.

James 5:13–20 is the final passage of the epistle. In her commentary on the passage Marie Isaacs writes: "Nowhere is the pastoral orientation of James more evident than in this concluding section."[1] When we read the Epistle of James, we get a glimpse into the life of the Church in the first century. James is a pastoral letter, addressed to our first-century spiritual ancestors. In reading the Epistle of James, it is as if we are sitting for instruction from one of the seminal pastors of the Church in its earliest days. In his commentary on our text Ralph Martin writes: "the reader enters a world of congregational relationships which embrace the entire spectrum of life's experiences, extending from gladness to sadness."[2] A keen observation. James 5:13–20 offers us a glimpse of life in the ancient world with its mixture of sadness and joy. Of course, our lives in the here and now are also inevitably a blend of difficult times and sad moments, balanced by easier times and moments—hopefully seasons of joy and happiness. It was true in the first century and it is true in the twenty-first century—congregational life touches on the entire spectrum of life experiences. In the last two-and-a-half weeks, five parishioners have died. In that same two-and-a-half week period, I have met with three different couples who are in the process of their premarital counseling. And in the same two-week period an infant was baptized. In the last two-and-a-half weeks, we in this parish family have experienced the circle of life. Last week I went to the home of parishioners to say goodbye to them as they were moving to a different state. Later in that same week, I went to the same neighborhood to welcome new parishioners into the life of St. Luke's.

Debbie and I have a friend in the United Kingdom whose name is Alison. When a new edition of our newsletter is published, I send Alison a hard copy. Yesterday, as I was checking my email, I found a message from Alison which read in part: "I particularly enjoyed your last parish magazine. The parish is clearly buzzing." From the UK, based on our newsletter: "The parish is clearly buzzing." In the midst of a pandemic.

I can only speak to the last eighteen years of history in this parish. While I did not know this congregation prior to 2003, I can tell you that in the last eighteen years this parish has never been more active than is now the case. We have never done more outreach. We have never offered more Christian Education. The 'footprint' of this parish is larger now than at any time in the last eighteen years. Again, this is true even in the midst of a pandemic. Consider this: Just imagine what we can do when we all get back together. If this parish can be so active and multi-faceted in the midst of a pandemic, just imagine what we can do when we finally clear the pandemic and most, if not all of our parishioners feel comfortable returning to in-person participation. But be that as it may, our parish is clearly buzzing, even now.

James 5:13–20 begins: "Are any among you suffering? They should pray. Are any cheerful? They should sing songs of praise." Then James continues: "Are any among you sick? They should call for the elders of the church and have them pray over them, anointing them with oil in the name of the Lord." And the passage goes on from there. We have here a glimpse into the life of a Christian congregation some 2,000 years ago, and then, as now, congregational life was a mixture of sharing each other's joys and pains. In this season of pandemic, our congregation has to come to grips with the realities of its pains and losses. We are to weep with those who weep. Amidst the pandemic, we have to come to grips with the dislocations that so many people have felt and are feeling. At the same time, people of faith must remember to be thankful for the many blessings that we continue to enjoy. Now more than ever it is important for us to remember to be grateful for so many blessings that, amidst the dislocations of the pandemic, can so easily be taken for granted if we are not mindful of remembering to give thanks.

I have said several times during this pandemic that if we have to go through it, I would much rather go through it now than at any other point in human history. Just think about the advances in science that have been made since the last global pandemic 100 years ago. We have so many promising treatment modalities on the horizon. And science has given us a safe and effective vaccine. If we have to experience a pandemic, I would much rather do it now than at any other time in human history. For all of the tools that we have in hand to fight this pandemic, we can be deeply grateful.

In thinking about this mix of pain and thankfulness I am reminded of the parable of the Laborers in the Vineyard, one of Jesus' more memorable parables.[3] You may remember the story. A landowner has a vineyard and he goes out at different times of the day to hire laborers. Some laborers work all day, but others work only a few hours. At the end of the day, all of the workers get paid the same. You may remember that those who had worked all day grumble at the fact that the others who worked less got paid the same wage. But in the end, the parable makes it clear that everyone has gotten what they were promised. John Claypool writes regarding this parable: "every one of the workers had an occasion for gratitude if they had only remembered what their circumstances were like before dawn."[4] An astute observation. It is understandable that the laborers who had worked all day grumbled when those who came in late got the same pay. But those who had worked all day got what they were promised. When they had awakened that morning, they were promised nothing. And thus Claypool's insight—every one of the workers had an occasion for gratitude if they would only remember what their circumstances were before dawn.

We can deal honestly with life's difficulties while at the same time remembering to look for its blessings. Even amidst this challenging season of pandemic we can remember to be grateful for the manifold blessings we continue to enjoy.

We began by talking about the life of the ancient Christian congregation(s) blessed to be on the receiving end of James' pastoral care. Let us now talk about our own congregation's life in the here and now. Early in the pandemic, for the better part of six months, we went to online worship only, moving to an altered worship schedule of one service at 10:00 a.m. on Sundays, Evening Prayer at 6:00 p.m. on Wednesdays, and the 12:10 p.m. service on Thursdays. These services were live-streamed with no in-person attendance save for essential staff. We did all of that because it was a practical necessity. We went to 'online only' because it was the only safe, responsible thing to do in the early days of the pandemic. So, to accomplish that goal, we rearranged the furniture a little bit. We moved the pulpit to the center of the choir. We set Isaac Doty's cell phone on a tripod in front of the pulpit and reimagined how to do church. The question before us was: How can St. Luke's continue to be St. Luke's in the throes of a pandemic?

Over time, we have evolved to using multiple cameras. We now have a soundboard. The production quality of our online offerings continues to improve, but in the beginning it was as rudimentary as it could be. And it was all out of practical necessity in order to keep the church alive and active. In the earliest stages of the pandemic, we were not thinking about how many parishioners we might gain from online worship. But then the comments started streaming in from places like Franklin, Tennessee; Canton, North Carolina; Betsy Lane, Kentucky; Yorkshire, England; Monrovia, Liberia. And California, Uganda, Australia, and everywhere in between. Slowly but surely, we began to realize that the practical necessity of online worship could actually be a tool, a resource, a vehicle for church growth. I will never forget the day we had back-to-back comments on our Facebook page, the first of which read: "I'm within half a mile of you, but have never attended your church before today." The very next comment read: "We're checking in from Costa Rica." Back-to-back! This is when we began to realize that the 'practical necessity' of online worship could come to be understood as an extraordinary opportunity to enable others from far and wide to participate in the life of this parish.

The Epistle of James offers us a priceless glimpse into the life of an early Christian congregation. When we read James we are, in effect, sitting with and receiving instruction from one of the great pastors of the early Christian Church, possibly Jesus' own brother. But as significant as the author of James is in Christian history—and he is—James could never have imagined in the first century that one day a small local church would have the ability to broadcast the Good News of Jesus Christ all over the world. James simply did not live in such a world, but we do. What started out with a cell phone on a tripod has now connected us to anyone, anywhere in the world who has a computer and wishes to participate in the life of this church. In the beginning of the pandemic, we were faced with the reality of the *necessity* of having to reimagine worship. Now we have the *opportunity* of reimagining how to do church via an electronic device small enough to fit in the palm of one's hand. Centuries-old geographic boundaries have simply vanished. Until the onset of the pandemic, St. Luke's rightly used to focus on Cleveland and Bradley County, with bits of Polk, Hamilton, Meigs, Rhea and McMinn counties thrown in. While we still focus on our local setting, we can also now reach out beyond our region to the rest of the world, and anyone in the rest of the world can find us. Going forward, the possibilities are seemingly endless.

A silver lining in this awful season of pandemic is that the reach of this church now very nearly knows no bounds. In staff meeting two weeks ago, Isaac's cell phone pinged, after which he offered: "That ping was my notification that someone in Japan is on our website." A few minutes later his phone pinged again, after which he informed us: "That was my notification that someone in Germany is on our website." Within thirty minutes, on a routine day, we got two notifications that people in Japan and in Germany were interacting in a meaningful way with St. Luke's Episcopal Church, Cleveland, Tennessee (https://www.stlukescleveland.org). Welcome to the church of the future. Amen.

---

1. Marie E. Isaacs, *Reading Hebrews and James: A Literary and Theological Commentary*. Reading the New Testament. Charles H. Talbert, General Editor (Macon, GA: Smyth and Helwys Publishing Inc., 2002), 246.
2. Ralph P. Martin, *James*. Word Biblical Commentary, Volume 48. David A. Hubbard and Glenn W. Barker, General Editors (Nashville: Nelson Reference and Electronic, 1998), 214.
3. Matthew 20:1–16.
4. John Claypool, *Stories Jesus Still Tells: The Parables*. Revised Second Edition (Cambridge, MA: Cowley Publications, 2000), 33.

31

THE SADDEST
VERSE IN THE BIBLE

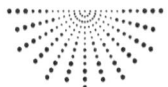

MARK 10:17–31 • 10 OCTOBER 2021
TWENTIETH SUNDAY AFTER PENTECOST

¹⁷As Jesus was setting out on a journey, a man ran up and knelt before him, and asked him, "Good Teacher, what must I do to inherit eternal life?" ¹⁸Jesus said to him, "Why do you call me good? No one is good but God alone. ¹⁹You know the commandments: 'You shall not murder; You shall not commit adultery; You shall not steal; You shall not bear false witness; You shall not defraud; Honor your father and mother.'" ²⁰He said to him, "Teacher, I have kept all these since my youth." ²¹Jesus, looking at him, loved him and said, "You lack one thing; go, sell what you own, and give the money to the poor, and you will have treasure in heaven; then come, follow me." ²²When he heard this, he was shocked and went away grieving, for he had many possessions. ²³Then Jesus looked around and said to his disciples, "How hard it will be for those who have wealth to enter the kingdom of God!" ²⁴And the disciples were perplexed at these words. But Jesus said to them again, "Children, how hard it is to enter the kingdom of God! ²⁵It is easier for a camel to go through the eye of a needle than for someone who is rich to enter the kingdom of God." ²⁶They were greatly astounded and

said to one another, "Then who can be saved?" ²⁷Jesus looked at them and said, "For mortals it is impossible, for not for God; for God all things are possible." ²⁸Peter began to say to him, "Look, we have left everything and followed you." ²⁹Jesus said, "Truly I tell you, there is no one who has left house or brothers or sisters or mother or father or children or fields, for my sake and for the sake of the good news, ³⁰who will not receive a hundredfold now in this age —houses, brothers and sisters, mothers and children, and fields with persecutions—and in the age to come eternal life. ³¹But many who are first will be last, and the last will be first."

~

All three writers of the Synoptic Gospels, Matthew, Mark and Luke, offer their own account of this encounter. This fact alone testifies to the significance of the event in the ministry of Jesus. Matthew tells us that this man was young (19:20). Luke tells us that he was a ruler (18:18). All three accounts agree that he was blessed with material possessions. Thus we have come to call him "the rich young ruler." Mark tells us that this man ran to Jesus and knelt before him—a clear sign of humility. And he asks what might be thought of as *the* spiritual question: "What must I do to inherit eternal life?" In context, "eternal life" here does not refer exclusively to the afterlife, but to a *quality of life* possible in the present as well as in eternity. Thus the man's question is not just about the future. He is also asking about the present. What must I do to find spiritual fulfillment? How do I find more quality of life, more spiritual vitality, in the here and now? *The* spiritual question: What must I do to inherit eternal life? Jesus' response is: "You know the commandments..." And the man's response is: "Teacher, I have kept all these since my youth." What this man seems to be saying is: "I am a good person. I live a good, moral life. But..." Something is missing.

Matthew tells us that this man was young. Luke tells us that he was a ruler. But it is only in Mark where we get this one other detail. Mark tells us that, having heard the young man's question, "Jesus, looking at him, loved him..." What Mark is clearly conveying here is that Jesus took this man's spiritual dilemma seriously. Jesus has truly heard the depth, the seriousness of the man's question. He took the time to look this young man in the eye and to 'see' him. We all want to be 'seen,' to be recognized in and for our individuality. We all want to be heard, and to be taken seriously.

Something especially encouraging happened for me earlier in the pandemic. Within a couple of weeks, I got two separate emails from two people speaking independently of each other. To my knowledge, these two parishioners do not even know each other. But in the thick of the pandemic, with all of its disruptions and challenges to parish life, within just a couple of weeks I heard it twice: "I see you." And that affirmation, that encouragement, was, and remains, life-giving. At that precise 'moment' in time, amidst all the challenges of pastoring a church through the unprecedented experience of online only—'remote' worship—it was exactly what I needed to hear. *I see you.*

In our passage, Mark is telling us that Jesus *saw* this man. He heard the man's question in all its earnestness. And to this one man, in this one moment, given this man's uniquely individual circumstances, Jesus had this response: "You lack one thing: go, sell what you own, and give the money to the poor...then come, follow me." "*You* (emphasis added) lack one thing..." Not just anyone could have picked up and left their family, or their work. But Jesus sensed that this young man had the means and the opportunity to leave his life behind, at least for a season. And to this one person, in this one moment, Jesus says: *Here is your answer. Sell your stuff, give the money to the poor, and come with us. If you really want the answer to your question, then come, follow me.*

We all know the truism: "Be careful what you ask for." Mark 10:22 has been referred to as the saddest verse in the Bible. A strong claim: *the* saddest verse in the Bible. "When he heard this, he was shocked and went away grieving, for he had many possessions." This man was invited by Jesus to be a disciple; he actually had the opportunity to follow, and to learn from Jesus himself. But in the end, he just could not do it. He could not remove himself from the sense of security that he gained from his possessions.

We all know that in real estate the three most important things are: location, location, location. And I think that in the interpretation of Scripture the three most important things are: context, context, context. Historical context. We must pay attention to the moment of history referenced in a biblical text. And we must also appreciate the literary context of a passage. We must have a sense of the author's intention in placing a passage in relationship with the other passages around it. Context, context, context. When we think about the rich young ruler, we have, whether we think about it consciously or not, 2,000 years of history at our disposal to process what happened. We have 2,000 years' worth of theological reflection at our disposal to know that this young man should have gone with Jesus. But 'Monday morning quarterbacking' is easy. By 'Monday morning,' it is easy to know what the player or coach should have done. But in the moment, critical decisions are always much harder to make without the benefit of hindsight. In real time, we simply do not always have the necessary perspective to make the right decision. So, we have to think in terms of historical context here with the rich young ruler. He was not *reflecting* on his encounter with Jesus, he was *in* it. And in the moment Jesus says to him: *If you really want your question answered, come with us. Follow me, and I will show you the way to eternal life.* But in the moment, the man could not separate himself from the security of his possessions. In the end, his possessions possessed him.

In his commentary on Mark 10:17–31, Larry Hurtado writes that this passage is intended: "to be read soberly by those who regard themselves as Jesus' followers."[1] Soberly. What does Jesus ask of *us*? What are *we* being asked to give up in order to follow Jesus faithfully? In commenting on the passage James A. Brooks notes: "Jesus did not teach that wealth is evil."[2] Nowhere does Jesus say that wealth, in and of itself, is inherently evil. We all know that wealth can be achieved by hard, dedicated, honest, and in some cases visionary, work. Brooks continues: "[Jesus] did not teach that poverty is better than riches."[3] It is incumbent upon us to acknowledge and respect the effects of grinding poverty, and we must be careful never to allow ourselves to glorify poverty, as if it would give us an inherently closer connection to God. Brooks continues: "[Jesus] did not teach that only the poor can be saved."[4] Of course, the love of God is poured out equally on all who will receive it. Brooks then concludes: "[Jesus] did teach that discipleship is costly..."[5] The fact that this man was rich was not an inherent spiritual hurdle. The fact that he had known success and comfort did not make him any more or less valuable to God than someone who was poor. But in the moment, Jesus perceived that this particular young man was actually able to drop what he was doing and literally join with the disciples in following. But in real time, he just could not bring himself to accept the invitation.

Life for us is in many ways markedly different than it was in first-century Palestine. The rich young ruler could not have imagined life as we experience it with the modern conveniences that most (though not all) of us enjoy. And yet, as the writer of Ecclesiastes says: "there is nothing new under the sun."[6] In the end, human beings are still human beings, and there is a baseline continuity from one generation to another. And though separated from the rich young ruler by 2,000 years of history, the same profound, potentially life-changing invitation comes to us down through the ages. "Come, follow me." Amen.

---

1. Larry W. Hurtado, *Mark*. New International Biblical Commentary. W. Ward Gasque, New Testament Editor (Peabody, MA: Hendrickson Publishers, Inc., 1989), 164.

2. James A. Brooks, *Mark*. The New American Commentary. Volume 23. David S. Dockery, General Editor (Nashville: B and H Publishing Group, 1991), 161.
3. *Ibid.*
4. *Ibid.*
5. *Ibid.*
6. Ecclesiastes 1:9b.

32
WIDENING THE CIRCLE

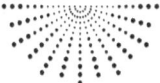

MARK 12:28–34 • 31 OCTOBER 2021
23RD SUNDAY AFTER PENTECOST

²⁸One of the scribes came near and heard them disputing with one another, and seeing that he answered them well, he asked him, "Which commandment is the first of all?" ²⁹Jesus answered, "The first is, 'Hear, O Israel: the Lord our God, the Lord is one; ³⁰you shall love the Lord your God with all your heart, and with all your soul, and with all your mind, and with all your strength.' ³¹The second is this, 'You shall love your neighbor as yourself.' There is no other commandment greater than these." ³²Then the scribe said to him, "You are right, Teacher; you have truly said that 'he is one, and besides him there is no other'; ³³and 'to love him with all the heart, and with all the understanding, and with all the strength,' and 'to love one's neighbor as oneself,'—this is much more important than all whole burnt offerings and sacrifices." ³⁴When Jesus saw that he answered wisely, he said to him, "You are not far from the kingdom of God." After that no one dared to ask him any question.

We all know what is meant by, "long story short." It means, "to make a long story short." And we know what we mean by, "cut to the chase," or, "let's get on with it," or, "where is this headed?" Sometimes in conversation we might say: "What is the gist of what you are trying to say?" I looked up the word "gist" this past week. One definition of gist is: "the main point of a matter."[1] The definition further includes, "essence."[2] What is the gist? What is the essence of the matter at hand?

"One of the scribes came near and heard them disputing with one another..." We have met others along the way in Mark 12 who enter into disputation with Jesus, several of whom are trying to trap him into giving the 'wrong' answer. In our culture, we might say that these people are looking for a "gotcha" moment. The scribe in 12:28, however, comes to Jesus in a different way. "Which commandment is the first of all?" What this scribe is doing is, in effect, saying: Let's cut to the chase. Tell us the gist of what you think. What is the essence of a moral life? In hearing the term "scribe," we might think "journalist." But in the biblical era a scribe was a lawyer, a specialist who dedicated his life to the study and the implementation of Jewish law. So, amidst all the disputations Mark records for us in chapter 12, this one scribe attempts to cut to the chase and get to the heart of the matter. He asks: "Which commandment is the first of all?" And Jesus' answer is straightforward: "'you shall love the Lord your God with all your heart, and with all your soul, and with all your mind, and with all your strength.'" And, "'You shall love your neighbor as yourself.'" And to put a fine point on it he adds: "There is no other commandment greater than these."

When we think about Jewish law in the biblical era we may instinctively think about the Ten Commandments, but over the hundreds of years between Moses and Jesus the rabbis had added to the Ten Commandments in order to sharpen them, to make them 'clearer,' to eliminate any ambiguity as to what the original Ten Commandments meant amidst all the varied realities of daily life. The gist here is that by the time of Jesus the original Ten

Commandments had been expanded to 613! Of the 613, 365 were phrased in the negative, "Thou shalt not...," while 248 were phrased in the positive, "Thou shalt..." So, the scribe in 12:28 succeeds in cutting to the chase. He is able to drill down to the essence of the matter. And so does Jesus.

Some of you will know the name Hillel (d. ca. AD 10), one of the great rabbis in the history of Judaism. Hillel and Jesus just missed each other. It is a tantalizing thought: Hillel and Jesus in conversation with each other—face to face. In one particularly instructive story from the life of Hillel, a Gentile approached him and said: "Explain to me the commandments while you are standing on one leg." That is a great way of framing the question, is it not? 'What would you tell me about the law while standing on one leg?' Which is, of course, a way of saying: Let's cut to the chase. What is the gist of the law? And here is what Hillel said: "What is hateful to you, do not do to your neighbor. That is the whole Torah while the rest is commentary."

The encounter between Jesus and this particular scribe in Mark 12:28–34 is recorded in all three Synoptic Gospels, which speaks to the importance of their conversation. Those who engage in disputation with Jesus earlier in Mark 12 seek to argue with him in order to trap him. They are adversarial, looking for a gotcha moment. But the scribe in our passage approaches Jesus in a fundamentally different way. He wishes to step back from the trees to see the forest. Which of the 613 precepts of the law mark its essence? Jesus' response could not have been clearer: Love God with your whole being, and love your neighbor as yourself. Everything else in the law is commentary.

In general terms, the scribes and the Pharisees do not come off very well in the Gospels. They tend to be on the wrong side of the discussion with Jesus. And thus it is helpful here to see a scribe portrayed in a positive light. Jesus says to him in 12:34: "You are not far from the kingdom of God." He is clearly positive towards this scribe. But far more often than not scribes and Pharisees are pictured negatively in the Gospels, and thus, if we are not careful, we may tend to see all of them negatively, as if every scribe and every Pharisee was always looking to find fault with Jesus. Of course, that is not what happened. Scribes and Pharisees were unique in their individuality just as we are. Scribes and Pharisees would have held different points of view, and, to be sure, there were scribes and Pharisees who saw Jesus in a positive light.

In commenting on our passage, Fred Craddock writes: "Law can lose its heart; ritual can lose its reason; a relationship can lose its love."[3] In the Gospels, *some* scribes and *some* Pharisees are pictured as being overly legalistic. In studying the letter of the law, *some* scribes and Pharisees lost sight of its spirit. But in our passage we see a markedly different portrait of a scribe who is clearly pictured in a positive light. And here we are all reminded to be wary of too easily using labels or categories to describe whole groups of people whom we do not know in their individuality. The scribe in our passage reminds us to be wary of painting with too broad a brush. Two millennia after the encounter between Jesus and this particular scribe was recorded by all three Synoptists, we are reminded in our time and place that behind labels and categories are *individuals—people like us—*made in the image and likeness of God. We are meant to engage with *people,* not with labels or categories. And, of course, whenever possible the best way to engage is face to face, eye to eye, heart to heart.

One of the great philosophers and theologians in the Western tradition is Søren Kierkegaard (1813–55). It is Kierkegaard who offers us this timeless wisdom: Once you label me, you negate me. In other words, once we place someone in a category, or reduce someone to a label, we then cease to interact with said person in his or her individuality. And once we do that, we lose sight of the individual. *Once you label me, you negate me.* Jesus frequently was criticized by the 'righteous' for interacting with the 'wrong' people. But he was undeterred in his mission always to be widening the circle of those who knew the grace, the mercy—the unconditional love of God. Amen.

1. *Webster's Ninth New Collegiate Dictionary.* Springfield, MA: Merriam-Webster Inc., Publishers, 1987), 518.
2. *Ibid.*
3. Fred B. Craddock, *Preaching Through the Christian Year (Year B): A Comprehensive Commentary on the Lectionary.* Fred B. Craddock, John H. Hayes, Carl R. Holladay, Gene M. Tucker, Contributors (Harrisburg, PA: Trinity Press International, 1993), 459.

33
THE VALUE OF TIME

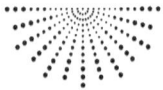

LUKE 21:25–36 • 28 NOVEMBER 2021
FIRST SUNDAY OF ADVENT

²⁵Jesus said, "There will be signs in the sun, the moon, and the stars, and on the earth distress among nations confused by the roaring of the sea and the waves. ²⁶People will faint from fear and foreboding of what is coming upon the world, for the powers of the heavens will be shaken. ²⁷Then they will see 'the Son of Man coming in a cloud' with power and great glory. ²⁸Now when these things begin to take place, stand up and raise your heads, because your redemption is drawing near." ²⁹Then he told them a parable: "Look at the fig tree and all the trees; ³⁰as soon as they sprout leaves you can see for yourselves and know that summer is already near. ³¹So also, when you see these things taking place, you know that the kingdom of God is near. ³²Truly I tell you, this generation will not pass away until all things have taken place. ³³Heaven and earth will pass away, but my words will not pass away. ³⁴Be on guard so that your hearts are not weighed down with dissipation and drunkenness and the worries of this life, and that day catch you unexpectedly, ³⁵like a trap. For it will come upon all who live on the face of the whole earth. ³⁶Be alert at all times, praying that you may have the

strength to escape all these things that will take place, and to stand before the Son of Man."

∼

During my junior and senior years in college I was a Resident Assistant. As part of the initial training to be an RA, my peers and I attended a time management workshop led by Jim Phillips, our Director of Campus Safety and Security. My recollection is that the workshop was well presented and beneficial. But all these years later, I do not remember a single word that Jim Phillips said.

What I do remember from the workshop is that it marked the occasion when, for the first time as an adult, I seriously considered the value of time. Twenty years old at that point, blessed with robust health and strength, I had never really been forced to consider the preciousness, the fragility—the *value*—of time. When we are young and blessed with good health, we too readily assume that time is on our side, that we are 'immortal.' But there does come that point in life when we start to realize that time is moving on, seemingly faster than ever before. There come those moments when we start to ask ourselves the question: Where does the time go?

In preparation for this address, I came across this statement by an anonymous author: "...time is always ending, passing away, subtracting from the length of our days." This observation has made a strong impression on me. For one thing, it is accurate. Time *is* always ending, passing away, subtracting from the length of our days, and thus at one level we have every reason to lament the passing of time. But I wish to balance this reality with something that I picked up several years ago. This insight comes from a cancer survivor who said in the midst of an interview: "Aging is a privilege." In that moment, those words hit me like a ton of bricks. They still do. *Aging is a privilege.* And thus while at one level we may recognize and lament the reality of the *passing* of time, at another level we are wise to recognize that we are blessed with the gift—the *grace*—of more time.

In my office there are only two photographs of me from my first pastorate. In one of those photos I am with a beloved parishioner who, at the time, was in her eighties while I was in my late twenties. Once in a while that photo catches my eye, and though my first thought is always of my memories of Lillian Sherman, I can never help but notice how young I was back then. I see that fresh face, and that head full of hair. And those shoulders! 'Those were the days.' In gazing at that photo from so long ago, a part of me cannot help but think: Those *were* the days. But, in reality, they were not. Even if I could, I would not go back. Because if I were to go back, I would have to give up all the learning that has taken place in the intervening years. If I went back, I would have to forego the maturity that the years have brought and continue to bring. If I were to go back, I would have to give up all the experiences that have gone into making me who I am. If I were to go back, I would not know Debbie. And if I were to go back, I would not know you. Time *is* always ending, passing away, subtracting from the length of our days. And yet... Aging *is* a privilege, and the 'passing' of time is, ultimately, a gift.

Another season of Advent is upon us: a new, fresh season in which to consider both the mystery of the Incarnation, and the promise of the Second Coming of Christ. Fleming Rutledge has a new book out. I saw an ad for it about a month ago and immediately went to my computer, to my Amazon account, to get the book on its way. The book is titled, *Means of Grace: A Year of Weekly Devotions*. In the book Rutledge talks about "formation." We Episcopalians tend to talk a lot about formation. We talk about it in terms of Christian education, and in terms of worship. Fleming Rutledge says regarding formation: "if there is one thing in addition to the Bible and the 1928 Book of Common Prayer that has 'formed' me, it is the church calendar."[1] I am really struck by that statement. Of course, the Bible. And yes, the Prayer Book. But she adds that the church calendar has formed her: Advent, Christmas, Epiphany, Lent, Easter, Pentecost... And she is right. The seasons do shape us. Over time, the seasons inform who we are. The liturgical calendar reminds us of the life cycle. Indeed, the liturgical calendar marks the cycle of life. We all experience different 'seasons' in our lives. There are different rhythms to our lives just as there are different rhythms to the church year.

In another reflection, Rutledge writes that Advent is, "the deepest place in the church year."[2] Indeed, Advent is meant to be experienced as the deepest place in the church year because of its *two* points of focus: the Incarnation—Christmas—and also the Second Coming of Christ. In Luke 21:34 Jesus says: "Be on guard..." And in 21:36: "Be alert..." In Advent we both commemorate the Incarnation and anticipate the promised Second Coming. Advent really is meant to be the deepest place in the church year. Week after week, in reciting the Nicene Creed we say: "For us and for our salvation he came down from heaven: by the power of the Holy Spirit he became incarnate from the Virgin Mary, and was made man."[3] We recall and affirm the theology of the Incarnation every week, no matter the time of year. And we also say this: "He will come again in glory to judge the living and the dead, and his kingdom will have no end."[4]

On this First Sunday of Advent, we once again enter into the deepest place in the Christian year. In a sermon for the First Sunday of Advent Mark Oakley observes: "We are very used to a Church that is loyal to the past. Where now is the Church that is loyal to the future?"[5] It is a probing and a haunting question. How do we maintain continuity with what has come before us and honor that continuity while, at the same time, recognizing that so much of life is ever evolving? While remaining grounded in, connected to, and guided by our Tradition(s), the Church is at the same time called to evolve and speak with a fresh voice to the moment that is now.

"Almighty God, give us grace to cast away the works of darkness, and put on the armor of light..."[6] Amen.

1. Fleming Rutledge, *Means of Grace: A Year of Weekly Devotions.* Laura Bardolph Hubers, Editor (Grand Rapids: William B. Eerdmans Publishing Company, 2021), xxii.
2. *Ibid.*, 3.
3. *The Book of Common Prayer* (New York: The Seabury Press, 1979), 358.
4. *Ibid.*, 359.
5. Mark Oakley, *By Way of the Heart: The Seasons of Faith* (Norwich: Canterbury Press, 2019), 2.
6. *The Book of Common Prayer,* 211.

34

THE DANCE OF CONTRITION AND JOY

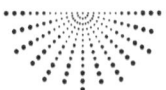

LUKE 3:1–6 • 5 DECEMBER 2021
SECOND SUNDAY OF ADVENT

¹In the fifteenth year of the reign of Emperor Tiberius, when Pontius Pilate was governor of Judea, and Herod was ruler of Galilee, and his brother Philip ruler of the region of Ituraea and Trachonitis, and Lysanias ruler of Abilene, ²during the high priesthood of Annas and Caiaphas, the word of God came to John son of Zechariah in the wilderness. ³He went into all the region around the Jordan, proclaiming a baptism of repentance for the forgiveness of sins, ⁴as it is written in the book of the words of the prophet Isaiah, "The voice of one crying out in the wilderness: 'Prepare the way of the Lord, make his paths straight. ⁵Every valley shall be filled, and every mountain and hill shall be made low, and the crooked shall be made straight, and the rough ways made smooth; ⁶and all flesh shall see the salvation of God.'"

∼

One of my mentors is a man named John Booty. John Everitt Booty was an Episcopal priest and church historian. In his prime, John Booty was the premier historian of

Anglican Christianity in the world. This high opinion of John is not mine alone. There came a point in his career when the General Convention of the Episcopal Church designated John as Historiographer of the Episcopal Church, Convention's way of acknowledging John's preeminence in his field.

In my second year of seminary at Sewanee I was assigned to be John Booty's research assistant, and so began one of the great formative experiences of my life. Prior to my time at Sewanee, when I was a graduate student at Emory, I was assigned to be research assistant for Carl Holladay, one of the great New Testament scholars in the world. I went two for two in the work-study lottery, and all these years later I remain grateful.

One of my lasting memories of John Booty is that he was as humble as anyone I have ever met in my life. For all his acclaim as a church historian, John could not have been a nicer person, nor more accessible, nor humbler.

John could be an eccentric, oftentimes fitting the stereotype of an absent-minded professor. An example. One of my fellow students at Sewanee was a woman named Susan. Susan was a late vocation to the priesthood and had been a working artist her entire career up until seminary. Given her regard for John, she painted a picture for him as a gift. In due course John had the painting framed and displayed prominently on a wall in his office, and once it was in place he asked Susan to come and take a look at it. On the day, I happened to be in the office before Susan got there, and John asked me of the painting: "What do you think it means? What do you think it represents?" I looked at the painting and replied: "I have no idea." He responded: "Neither do I." So, a few minutes later Susan came in and, upon seeing the painting hanging on the wall, her jaw dropped. She then said: "It's upside down! You've had it framed upside down."

Of all the professors of theology I ever had in college, graduate school and seminary, and in all my post-graduate work, John Booty is the only professor I ever had who started every class session with prayer. You may have noticed over the years that every class session I teach starts with prayer. I learned that practice from John Booty, and I carry it forward to this day.

For all that I learned from John Booty, what sticks in my memory most of all is this one-liner: "Liturgy is the dance of contrition and joy." I have never forgotten it. *Liturgy is the dance of contrition and joy.* We get to that point in the liturgy every week when we say: "Most merciful God, we confess that we have sinned against you in thought, word, and deed, by what we have done, and by what we have left undone. We have not loved you with our whole heart; we have not loved our neighbors as ourselves. We are truly sorry and we humbly repent."[1] Each week contrition is a central part of our worship. *We are truly sorry and we humbly repent.*

In introducing the prophetic ministry of John the Baptist, Luke tells us that John went into all the region around the Jordan proclaiming a baptism of repentance for the forgiveness of sins. John's message of repentance was framed in the context of baptism. Both John the Baptist and Jesus would have spoken Aramaic in their everyday conversations. Aramaic is a Semitic language, similar to but not quite the same as Hebrew. But by the time the Gospels were written in the second half of the first century, Greek was the most common language among the Gospels' readers and hearers, and thus the Gospel writers wrote in Greek. The Greek word for repentance is *metanoia*. In the New Testament, *metanoia*, "repentance," means "a change of mind." To repent is to have a change of mind. The biblical word *metanoia* was derived from an everyday Greek word that meant, "to turn around." When we talk about repentance in its New Testament context, what we are really talking about is a change of mind, a change of direction. Or, as we might frame it in *our* everyday language, a change of heart. And in this change of mind, this *metanoia*, what we are really talking about is turning around. We are *truly sorry* and we *humbly repent.*

In commenting on our passage, Sharon Ringe describes repentance as being: "a reorientation of one's life on a new course."[2] We commit to a reorientation every time we repent and receive forgiveness. It is a strong term—*reorientation*.

GPS technology has become ubiquitous for most of us. While driving, when we choose a route different than the one suggested by GPS, what happens? The GPS has to adjust, and the system sends us a message: "Recalculating." *Recalculating*. And that is what repentance allows us: a turn, a shift, a change. How many times over the years have we wished for a fresh start? A clean slate? A new beginning? The truth is, it is there for the taking at all times and in all places.

In commenting on our passage Fleming Rutledge notes: "repentance does not mean just being sorry...*metanoia* means to turn around, to reorient oneself in another direction. It means to receive a new start altogether."[3] Such instructive phrasing by one of the finest preachers of our time. Repentance and forgiveness open up the possibility of a new start altogether, a clean slate. God's grace offers us a fresh start if we will allow ourselves to receive such an extraordinary gift—*unconditional* love and forgiveness.

N. T. Wright notes regarding our passage: "All spiritual advance begins with a turning away from what is hindering our obedience."[4] This is what repentance offers us—spiritual advance —an open door to a new beginning.

Sunday after Sunday we come to that point in our liturgy when we say: "We are truly sorry and we humbly repent." But we do not stop there, do we? What comes next? "For the sake of your Son Jesus Christ, have mercy on us and forgive us; that we may *delight in your will* (emphasis added), and walk in your ways..."[5] Here again, this notion of turning, and the promise of change. So again, in the words of Fleming Rutledge: "repentance does not mean just being sorry...The Greek word *metanoia* means to turn around, to reorient oneself in another direction. It means to receive a new start altogether."

And, again, in those most memorable words of John Booty: "Liturgy is the dance of contrition and joy." Amen.

1. *The Book of Common Prayer* (New York: The Seabury Press, 1979), 360.
2. Sharon H. Ringe, *Luke*. Westminster Bible Companion. Patrick D. Miller and David L. Bartlett, Series Editors (Louisville: Westminster John Knox Press, 1995), 52.
3. Fleming Rutledge, *Means of Grace: A Year of Weekly Devotions*. Laura Bardolph Hubers, Editor (Grand Rapids: William B. Eerdmans Publishing Company, 2021), 8.
4. N. T. Wright, *Luke for Everyone* (Louisville: Westminster John Knox Press, 2004), 8.
5. *The Book of Common Prayer*, 360.

35
A MOMENT OF TRUTH

LUKE 3:7–18 • 12 DECEMBER 2021
THIRD SUNDAY OF ADVENT

⁷John said to the crowds that came out to be baptized by him, "You brood of vipers! Who warned you to flee from the wrath to come? ⁸Bear fruits worthy of repentance. Do not begin to say to yourselves, 'We have Abraham as our ancestor'; for I tell you, God is able from these stones to raise up children to Abraham. ⁹Even now the axe is lying at the root of the trees; every tree therefore that does not bear good fruit is cut down and thrown into the fire." ¹⁰And the crowds asked him, "What then should we do?" ¹¹In reply he said to them, "Whoever has two coats must share with anyone who has none; and whoever has food must do likewise." ¹²Even tax collectors came to be baptized, and they asked him, "Teacher, what should we do?" ¹³He said to them, "Collect no more than the amount prescribed for you." ¹⁴Soldiers also asked him, "And we, what should we do?" He said to them, "Do not extort money from anyone by threats or false accusation, and be satisfied with your wages." ¹⁵As the people were filled with expectation, and all were questioning in their hearts concerning John, whether he might be the Messiah, ¹⁶John answered all of them by saying, "I baptize you with water;

but one who is more powerful than I is coming; I am not worthy to untie the thong of his sandals. He will baptize you with the Holy Spirit and fire. [17]His winnowing fork is in his hand, to clear his threshing floor and to gather the wheat into his granary; but the chaff he will burn with unquenchable fire." [18]So, with many other exhortations, he proclaimed the good news to the people.

~

In an Advent sermon Fleming Rutledge says of John the Baptist: "He is the last and greatest of the Hebrew prophets..."[1] As followers of Christ, we may instinctively think of John as the first Christian prophet. And at one level that is true. But we have to remember that John was preaching before Jesus was baptized, and thus it is true that he can be seen as both the last and greatest of the Hebrew prophets and the first Christian prophet.

The Anglican priest and spiritual writer Michael Mayne says of John the Baptist that he is a "disturbing and disruptive" figure.[2] Mayne adds: "there is a thin line between the prophet and the fanatic. The prophet is one who discerns the signs of the times and by standing against the grain of popular opinion points to truths the rest of us miss."[3] There is indeed a thin line between the prophet and the fanatic. In real time, prophets tend to be thought of as troublemakers, agitators. At least as often as not it takes hindsight, it takes perspective, to see that the troublemakers, the agitators—the prophets—were right. In his time, John the Baptist was both disturbing and disruptive.

I have never started a sermon with, "You brood of vipers." I never have, nor do I ever intend to. But John meant to. He *was* disturbing and disruptive. He meant to challenge his audience. He challenged the status quo. It is true that our faith is meant to comfort us and to reassure us when we need comfort and reassurance. But our faith is also meant to challenge us. The life of faith is meant to move us forward, closer and closer to the will and the heart of God. And we do need prophetic voices, sometimes quietly persistent, sometimes loud and agitating. There are times when we need to be challenged—as individuals, as a church, and as a culture. These are teachable moments through which we are meant to be moved forward in our understanding of the truth. And thus prophetic voices like John's are necessary. He was necessary, and the prophets of our own time are necessary as well. Sometimes we need a nudge, a push or a prod(!) to get us moving in the right direction.

John drew large crowds preaching a baptism of repentance for the forgiveness of sins. His was a 'new' message in real time, a revival of prophecy. And thus, people were asking him: What does this mean? What should we do? In due course, Jesus was asked the same questions.

There came that moment when Jesus was asked: "Teacher, which commandment in the law is the greatest?"[4] A bit of historical context helps here. By the time of Jesus, the original Ten Commandments had been expanded by the rabbinic tradition to 613! Thus it was doubtless on the minds of many: Which is the greatest of the commandments? You may remember Jesus' answer. We call it the Summary of the Law. Jesus said: "'You shall love the Lord your God with all your heart, and with all your soul, and with all your mind.' This is the greatest and first commandment. And a second is like it: 'You shall love your neighbor as yourself.' On these two commandments hang all the law and the prophets."[5] And thus, 613 were whittled down to two. No wonder Jesus' message found a welcoming audience!

Full disclosure, I am not wearing camel's hair underneath these vestments! And I had my usual fried bologna and egg sandwich this morning, not locusts and wild honey. John the Baptist *was* an ascetic, a disturbing and disruptive figure if there ever was one. And yet the crowds kept going out to him. The Gospels make it clear that John's message found a welcoming audience.

We need prophets. We needed John the Baptist. People knew

that for all his disturbing and disruptions—for all the discomfort that his message caused—people knew that the Spirit of God was at work in him. And though they are easier to recognize with hindsight rather than in real time, prophets are among us still.

In describing John's call to repentance, Fred Craddock says that what he was doing was calling for "a moment of truth..."[6] And we are now living in one of those moments. The last few years have given us so much to ponder, to reckon with, and to be nudged, pushed, or prodded forward by in lastingly significant ways.

A brief story. Most of you have been in my office. Those of you who have may remember that the inside of my door is festooned with quotations or clippings on one thing or another. They are all meaningful to me. They may seem an indecipherable hodgepodge, but to me everything on that door has meaning; every clipping or quotation on that door represents for me a moment of insight and, in some meaningful way, progress. Everything collected on that door has, in its way, been life-changing for me. In preparing for this address I thought about a couple of those quotations. "Practice having no ego and you will be free" changed my life. The challenge is to remember it. "Love one another and you will be happy; it is as easy and as difficult as that" is life-changing. The trick is to remember. And of course there is: "The main thing is to keep the main thing the main thing." I found another life-changing quotation this past week. In the context of Advent, with thoughts of John the Baptist on my mind, and given where I am in my life right now, what I am about to share with you hit me like a ton of bricks this past week. To me, it frames perfectly John the Baptist's message of judgment *and* mercy. And it frames Advent perfectly. It is going up on the door this week, but in the meantime, I now offer it to you: "When repentance and forgiveness are available, judgment then is good news. The primary aim, after all, is to save the wheat, not to burn the chaff."[7] Amen.

1. Fleming Rutledge, *Advent: The Once and Future Coming of Jesus Christ* (Grand Rapids: William B. Eerdmans Publishing Company, 2018), 322.
2. Michael Mayne, *Responding to the Light: Reflections on Advent, Christmas and Epiphany*. Joel W. Huffstetler, Editor (Norwich: Canterbury Press, 2017), 16.
3. *Ibid*.
4. Matthew 22:36.
5. Matthew 22:37-40.
6. Fred B. Craddock, "Luke 3:7-18." *Preaching Through the Christian Year (Year C): A Comprehensive Commentary on the Lectionary*. Fred B. Craddock, John H. Hayes, Carl R. Holladay, Gene M. Tucker, Contributors (Valley Forge, PA: Trinity Press International, 1994), 18.
7. Fred B. Craddock, *Luke*. Interpretation: A Bible Commentary for Teaching and Preaching. James L. Mays, Series Editor (Louisville: Westminster John Knox Press, 1990), 49.

36
THE SLENDER THREAD OF MARY'S RESPONSE

LUKE 1:39–45 • 19 DECEMBER 2021
FOURTH SUNDAY OF ADVENT

³⁹In those days Mary set out and went with haste to a Judean town in the hill country, ⁴⁰where she entered the house of Zechariah and greeted Elizabeth. ⁴¹When Elizabeth heard Mary's greeting, the child leaped in her womb. And Elizabeth was filled with the Holy Spirit ⁴²and exclaimed with a loud cry, "Blessed are you among women, and blessed is the fruit of your womb. ⁴³And why has this happened to me, that the mother of my Lord comes to me? ⁴⁴For as soon as I heard the sound of your greeting, the child in my womb leaped for joy. ⁴⁵And blessed is she who believed that there would be a fulfillment of what was spoken to her by the Lord."

∽

In an Advent sermon on Luke 1:39–45 Michael Mayne remembers: "I was once in a group who were talking about a man whose integrity and singleness of purpose and very practical goodness had impressed us all. When we had finished discussing him an elderly woman who had remained silent said: 'Well, he must have had a very remarkable mother.'"[1]

Mary was the first human being to love Jesus. We contemporary Christians take our place among the countless millions over time who have loved Jesus, but Mary was the *first* human being to love our Lord, and thus her crucially important place in Christian history, theology, and spirituality. It is said that there are more Christian churches throughout the world named for Mary than for any other saint. And though it is true that Marian devotions are more prominent in the Roman Catholic Church, Mary certainly has her honored place within Anglicanism. Week after week, Anglicans join with other Christians the world over in reciting the Nicene Creed as part of our worship, and there comes that moment when we say: "by the power of the Holy Spirit he became incarnate from the Virgin Mary..."[2] Every week, Christians around the world are reminded of the crucial importance of Mary. We remember Mary for the fact that she gave birth to Jesus, and for this reason alone she is rightly honored among all Christians. But at a deeper, more spiritual level, we venerate Mary because of her faithful response to the Divine call.

We have 2,000 years' worth of hindsight to help us put Mary in perspective. We know how her story ends. But in real time, what would it have been like for a young woman from an ordinary family in a seemingly ordinary place to receive a message from the angel? "Do not be afraid, Mary, for you have found favor with God."[3] *We* see all of this from the vantage point of history. We know how her story plays out. But, in the moment, Mary did not. She could not have known. We can only try to imagine just how mysterious those months of pregnancy would prove to be for her: the unknown, the wonder, and, no doubt, the fear. And yet —in real time—she answered: "Here am I, the servant of the Lord; let it be with me according to your word."[4] In the aforementioned Advent sermon, Michael Mayne notes: "so much of the world's joy hangs on the slender thread of Mary's response."[5]

What about the importance of our responses in our everyday, seemingly ordinary lives? Moment to moment, hour to hour, day to day, how many choices are ours to make? Many of those choices are seemingly mundane, so much so that we may hardly even think about them. But we are, in fact, faced with myriad choices on a daily basis. And the question ever before us is: How do we respond? Mindlessly? Selfishly? Or, inspired and guided by the light of Christ?

Later on today, four children will be baptized in this church, and, as always, the Baptismal Covenant will be a key component of that liturgy. The Baptismal Covenant starts with a series of affirmations which call to mind the Creed. Then the Covenant moves on to a series of questions which begin with: "Will you...?" Will you stay active in church life? Will you come to the table regularly? Will you be faithful in your study of the Bible and in your prayers? And then we are asked: "Will you strive for justice and peace among all people, and respect the dignity of every human being?"[6] It is a profound commitment that we make when we choose to respond: "I will, with God's help."[7] I *will* come to the table regularly. I *will* study the Bible regularly. I *will* be faithful in my prayers. I will *strive* for justice and peace among all people, and will respect the dignity of *every* human being. These are haunting choices set before us every day: to *this* or *that* person, in *this* or *that* situation. To what we see on television, and on social media. How do we respond?

Of course, Mary is important to Christian history. But she is important to us in our everyday walk as well. In real time, her answer to the angel was: *Here am I, the servant of the Lord; let it be with me according to your word.*

Today is the Fourth Sunday of Advent. Christmas is almost here. However this season of Advent has gone for us up to now, there is yet time to ponder the faithfulness of Mary, and her role in God's gift to us: Christ our light. Mary is the first human being to have loved our Lord. Now it is our turn.

> Purify our conscience, Almighty God, by your daily visitation, that your Son Jesus Christ, at his coming, may find in us a mansion prepared for himself; who lives and reigns with you, in

the unity of the Holy Spirit, one God, now and forever. Amen.[8]

---

1. Michael Mayne, *Responding to the Light: Reflections on Advent, Christmas and Epiphany.* Joel W. Huffstetler, Editor (Norwich: Canterbury Press, 2017), 26.
2. *The Book of Common Prayer* (New York: The Seabury Press, 1979), 358.
3. Luke 1:30.
4. Luke 1:38.
5. Mayne, 26.
6. *The Book of Common Prayer,* 305.
7. *Ibid.*
8. *Ibid.,* 212.

ACKNOWLEDGMENTS

Thanks to the parishioners of St. Luke's Episcopal Church in Cleveland, Tennessee, who heard the addresses contained in this volume offered in their original form. To both our in-person and online congregations, you have my lasting gratitude for allowing me to walk with you through an unforgettable time.

Thanks to both Andrea Spraggins and Isaac Doty, my colleagues in ministry and friends, for your invaluable support of my work on these addresses in both their original and revised forms.

Thanks to Carl Holladay, Brian Cole, Brenda Orcutt, Jeff Ringer, Denise King, and Wesley Wachob for your gracious support of this book, and for our friendship.

Thanks to John R. Mabry of Apocryphile Press for your acceptance and support of this project, and for our friendship.

Thanks to my mother, Rachel Huffstetler, and my late father, Joe Huffstetler, for instilling in me a love of Scripture and the recognition of its primacy in matters of faith.

Sandy and Gary Farlow were the first parishioners of St. Luke's who said the words: "You should publish your sermons." I have not forgotten. Thank you.

Following my final time leading Bible study in St. Andrew's Episcopal Church, Canton, North Carolina, Marylin Nicholls looked at her young priest and said, "I look forward to reading your books." The memory brings tears to my eyes. Marylin, I hope you like this one.

Thanks to our dear friends Marilyn and Al Hoke. The

majority of the early work on this collection was done at your kitchen table at Alys. Looking forward to our meet up in Shelby!

In the end, deepest thanks go to my wife Debbie for your tireless support of and involvement with this project at every stage, including your invaluable editorial suggestions and the occasional tweak regarding content, and for typing seemingly endless versions of the 'final' draft. Thank you, my love. And now, OUR ADVENTURE continues.

ABOUT THE AUTHOR

Joel W. Huffstetler is Rector of St. Luke's Episcopal Church in Cleveland, Tennessee. Ordained in 1990, he previously served as Assistant to the Rector of St. Paul's Episcopal Church, Chattanooga, Tennessee, and as Rector of St. Andrew's Episcopal Church, Canton, North Carolina. He is the author or editor of fourteen books, including, *Practical Faith and Active Love: Meditations on the Epistle of James* (2020), and *Changed Eyes: Pandemic, Protests, Proclamation* (2023), both by Apocryphile Press, and numerous articles and reviews. He and his wife Debbie live in Cleveland, Tennessee.

www.ingramcontent.com/pod-product-compliance
Lightning Source LLC
Chambersburg PA
CBHW030854170426
43193CB00009BA/606